BOOK

WRITING

GUIDE FOR

TEENS

WRITE A BOOK WHILE IN SCHOOL

JERRY MINCHEY

Contents

Chapter 1
Introduction

"The difference between fiction and reality? Fiction has to make sense."

~ Tom Clancy

Whether you're in middle school, high school, or college, you can and should write and publish a book.

You can do it and have your book in your hands within 90 days.

The purpose of this book is simple. I want to convince you that you should write a book and then show you how easy it is to do so with today's technology. I'll also show you step-by-step how to write, publish, and market your book.

When is the best time to write and publish your book? Last year was the best time, but now is the second best.

If you're like I was when I was in school, I didn't even want to think about having to write a term paper or even a book report. The idea that it could be a fun project would have been the last thing that came to mind.

Write a book, and you'll be a rock star—well, almost

Consider how you would feel about yourself after writing and publishing a book. Your self-confidence would be through the roof. I'm sure none of your friends or classmates have ever written and published a book. I doubt if any of your teachers have either.

You will be one in a million when you're a teenager who has written and published a book.

Whether you're trying to get into college, get a job, get a promotion, or get a date, writing a book makes you special. A lot of people say they have thought about writing a book, but you'll stand out from the crowd because you have done more than think about it. You've taken action and done it. You've made it happen.

Write a book, and you'll have an income forever

When you write your book, Amazon will keep selling it for you year after year. Think about having several hundred dollars coming in every month while you do nothing.

My first book earned me over $75,000, and my second one brought in over $50,000. The best part is that the money continues to come in every month. I have written 30 books and don't plan to stop.

Warren Buffett said it best: *"If you don't find a way to make money while you sleep, you'll work until you die."*

Not all of my books have been super successful, but they've all made me money and continue to bring in more money every month.

Think about what you could do with a few hundred dollars coming in every month. You could make a car payment, buy a new computer, buy a lot of new clothes, travel, or maybe save some money to help pay for college.

Writing a book can change your life

Stephen King worked as a janitor and pumped gas to earn money before he started earning a living as a writer. He now makes over 90 million dollars a year from his writing.

J.K. Rowling is a British author famous for writing the Harry Potter series. Five years before writing *Harry Potter*, she was living on state welfare. Now, she has made over a **billion dollars** from writing books.

You probably don't need an outline

Some fiction writers start by writing a detailed outline, and most beginning writers think they have to have one. However, many of the best writers I know don't work from an outline. Stephen King doesn't use one.

Maybe you have a vague idea about what will happen in your story or the general direction your story will go.

That's fine but be prepared for things to go in a different direction. You never know what your characters are going to decide to do. After all, they each have a mind of their own. You're just telling the story of what they did.

If the writer is surprised by a character's actions, the readers will be, too. Many fiction writers tell me they usually don't know what will happen on the next page.

When you write without an outline, you'll have to do a lot of editing. You'll write things out of order, ramble a lot, repeat some information, and maybe forget to include something important. That's alright.

If you don't need to do much editing, it means you were being too critical of your writing as you went along and were not letting your thoughts flow freely.

The more you get to know your characters, the easier it is to write without an outline.

Think of Mark Twain's story about Huck Finn floating down the Mississippi River on a raft. Maybe he had it all planned out, but it's easy to see that if you knew Huck Finn well, you could write a story about him and let it develop as he floated down the river. Maybe Mark Twain didn't even know what was around the next bend of the river or what was going to happen next.

Amazon has made writing and publishing a book easier than ever

Publishing a book now is easy. It's not like it was a few years ago. In the old days, you would need an agent, an editor, a publisher, and a lot of money to publish a book. Now, you can do everything yourself and publish your book for zero cost.

Amazon's Kindle Direct Publishing (known as KDP) makes all this possible.

Writing a book is not one big monster of a leap—it's 101 small steps. You won't regret writing a book—even if it doesn't become a huge success—but you will regret *not* writing one.

Most people who think about writing a book overthink first and act later. And many of them never get around to acting (that is, writing) at all.

Every successful writer I know acted first and figured it out later. When you're writing your book, you'll have super-productive days and days when you delete more than you write. Have a sense of humor and remember what Scarlett O'Hara said in the movie and book *Gone with the Wind*, "Tomorrow is another day."

In the following chapters, I'll show you step-by-step how to make your book a reality.

Note: This chapter focuses on writing a novel. In Chapter 17, I'll explain how to write a nonfiction book. While a nonfiction book is easier to write, a novel would probably be more fun. You might decide to write one of each.

The main takeaway from this chapter: The purpose of this book is to convince you that you should write a book and then show you how to write and publish your first book. If you go about it the right way, writing a book will be fun and won't take years (or even months).

Chapter 2
Why You Should Write a Book

"He who dares not offend cannot be honest."

~ Thomas Paine

If three birds were sitting on a fence, and one of them decided to fly away, how many would be left?

If birds are anything like people, there's a good chance that three birds would still be on the fence. Just because one bird decided to fly away doesn't mean he really did. People decide to do things all the time and then never do anything.

The same applies to writing a book. In 2002, a *New York Times* survey found that 81% of Americans said they wanted to write a book.

However, another survey found that fewer than 15% of the people who said they wanted to write a book had ever written a single word. Fewer than 6% of those people had made any significant progress in writing a book, and less than 1% had finished writing a book. Most of those never published their book.

If you write and publish a book, you'll have accomplished what most people only dream about.

Reasons to write a book

There are several good reasons why you should write a book and why you should do it now while you're in school. Don't wait to do it someday.

Here are some of those reasons:

- **Writing a book will force you to be curious about the world around you.** You've heard it said that curiosity killed the cat, but that didn't happen—it made him happier. Several studies have confirmed that curiosity increases dopamine, which makes you feel happier with less anxiety and stress.

- **Writing a book will give you a purpose in life.** When you write about a topic or situation you're passionate about, you'll get fully involved, and your life will have more drive and momentum.

- **Writing a book can boost confidence.** As you progress toward finishing your book, you'll be amazed at how confident you feel. You'll feel even more confident when you've finished it and published it, and the sales commissions start coming in.

- **Writing a book will force you to trust yourself and your capabilities.** You might even call it a journey of self-growth. Why shouldn't you trust yourself and your capabilities? After all, you've written and published a book.

- **Write a book, and you'll have income forever.** If you write a good nonfiction book that solves a problem or an intriguing novel, you can make a ton of money. The money will continue to come in for years and years. Writing books could be an enjoyable and profitable side hustle or a full-time business.

- **Write a book and change your life.** If you can write one book, you can write another one. Your second book will be even easier to write because you won't have so many new things to learn. And your life can change when you can write books and bring in a steady stream of income.

Whether you want to write books as a full-time job, a side hustle, or just a hobby, being able to write and publish books will give you income, prestige, and freedom. When you become an author, people will think you know a whole lot more than you do. Let them keep thinking that.

When you can make money writing books, it gives you unlimited freedom. That's why it's true that writing a book can change your life.

How to make all of this happen

I'm convinced you can write a book that will change and enrich lives—the lives of the people who read your book and your own.

A recent Harvard Business Study determined two things you need to do to succeed at anything. Here are those two things:

#1. Those with a defined goal are 10 times more likely to succeed than those without.

#2. Those who write their goal down and see it every day are more likely to achieve their goal than those who set goals but don't write them down.

If your goal is to write a book, write it down in a place where you'll see it every day. Write down the date your book will be finished. Saying that you're going to write a book someday is not a goal.

Your completion date needs to be aggressive but realistic. Don't say you're going to finish your book in three weeks or three years. Three weeks is not realistic, and if you say three years, it means your heart's not in it. Three months might be a reasonable goal, depending on what else is going on in your life.

The main takeaway from this chapter: You have a story to tell, and the world needs your book. That's why you need to write a book. No one else can tell the story you and your characters can tell because they haven't lived it, but you and your characters have. As long as you feel your story will entertain people or change their lives, you must get busy and start writing it.

Chapter 3
If You Don't Have Time to Write

"I only write when inspiration strikes. Fortunately, it strikes at nine every morning."

~ William Faulkner

Consider this if you're thinking about writing a book but don't know where you would find the time.

You don't *find* time to write—you *make* time to write.

You have plenty of time to write

Everyone has the same 1,440 minutes in a 24-hour day. If you think you don't have time to write, it's because writing is not as important to you as other things in your life.

Your mindset is important. If you enjoy writing, you'll find time to do it. If you don't, you'll find excuses not to.

Benjamin Franklin said, "He that is good for making excuses is seldom good for anything else."

Look at all the things you're doing in your day and decide if they're all more important than writing your book. I'm sure some of the things are. But if you can't find some things to move to a lower priority so writing your book can move up the list, face the fact that writing is not a high priority in your life, and writing your book is not going to happen. It's that simple.

But before you forget about writing your book, ask yourself if watching TV, texting your friends, or posting comments on Facebook or TikTok is more important to you than writing your book. It's your choice. You can continue doing these things, or you can write your book.

To come up with the time to write, you have to assign writing a higher priority in your life than some of the other things you're doing.

J.K. Rowling had a job and kids. She also had to do everything everyone else had to do to keep their lives and house operating, but she was able to make time to write her Harry Potter series.

She said, "Be ruthless about protecting writing time. Some people don't seem to grasp that I have to sit down in peace and write the books. They apparently believe they spring up like mushrooms."

What are you willing to give up to make your book a reality?

Every minute of your day is already full, so if you want to write a book, you'll have to sacrifice something.

Writing time is not going to fall out of the sky. You're going to have to give up some of the things you're doing now to make time to write your book.

When you're thinking about giving up some things, you don't have to give them up forever—just until you finish writing your book.

The three biggest blocks of time you can free up would probably be to eliminate all—or at least most of—the time you spend watching TV, talking (and texting) with your friends, and surfing the Internet.

You could get up an hour earlier every morning

First thing in the morning is my most creative and productive time. Getting up an hour earlier doesn't mean you have to sleep an hour less. You can go to bed an hour earlier and then get up an hour earlier and write.

If you think you can't adjust your sleep schedule to do that, stop and think about it. Adjusting to the new schedule doesn't take long when daylight savings time rolls around every year. Setting your clocks ahead one hour means you're getting up an hour earlier. Resetting the clocks is just a way to help trick your brain. It's all in your head.

Get away from distractions

You can be much more productive when you can go somewhere away from all the distractions of your daily life.

Many famous writers have a special place they go to write. It's away from their daily distractions.

Could you find a way to make this work? Maybe you could close the door to your room and put a "Do not disturb" sign on it. That would only work if your family members take your request for alone time seriously.

Try to convince them you don't want to be interrupted, whether you're studying or writing. To make the technique work, don't abuse it by always leaving the sign on the door. If you can't block out all the noise, consider getting some noise-canceling headphones.

You can be a lot more productive if you have a quiet place to write away from distractions. That's one of the advantages of getting up early and doing your writing. Usually, it's quiet and without distractions.

Have a writing routine

If you plan on writing when you have time, you'll find that not much writing will get done. To be productive, you need to have a routine and stick to it. You don't have to follow this schedule for the rest of your life, but you can do it for 30, 60, or 90 days until you finish writing your book.

Ernest Hemingway was not available until noon every morning. He did a lot of socializing in the afternoons and evenings (some say way too much), but he was always back at his desk writing until noon the next morning.

Setting a deadline will help make things happen

You may never finish your book if you only write when you have time. But if you say, "I'll have the first draft finished in sixty days," or "I'll write five hundred words a day," there's a much better chance you'll do whatever it takes to meet your self-imposed goal. Even if you don't meet your goal, you'll get a lot closer to it than if you didn't set one.

The main takeaway from this chapter: This chapter shows you several things you can do to make time to write your book. If you decide not to write a book, accept that the reason is because it wasn't important to you. Don't cop out and say it's because you don't have time.

Chapter 4
Selecting a Killer Title

"The future never comes. Life is always now."

~ Eckhart Tolle

My favorite college English professor was Doctor Lee (affectionately known as Doc Lee). One of the few things I remember from her classes is that when we had to write a paper, she would always tell us, "It's your baby—name it."

I'll tell you the same thing, but I'll also show you some things that will help you name your baby.

The titles of a novel and a nonfiction book serve distinctly different purposes and how you develop them is different. In this chapter, I'll explain how to create titles for fiction and nonfiction books.

I'll discuss how to write a nonfiction book (including how to create the title) in Chapter 17, but for now, let me say that the purpose of a nonfiction book's title (and subtitle) is to make a bold promise to solve the readers' problem. That's not the case for a novel.

People buy nonfiction books to solve a problem, but they buy novels to be entertained

The purpose of a novel's title is not to tell the readers what the book is about but to intrigue them. Often, the title of a novel doesn't mean anything to the readers until after they've read the book.

For example, the title of the famous book and movie *Gone with the Wind* makes sense after you've read the book or seen the movie, but before you've read the book, you might think it would be about an adventure on a sailboat rather than something to do with the Civil War.

Look at Amazon's list of the 100 best-selling books to give you ideas and help you come up with a title for your book.

Note that most novels don't have subtitles, but nonfiction books always have subtitles.

Your title is the most important part of a nonfiction book

It's not as important for a novel, but it's still important.

Your nonfiction book's title is the key to successfully marketing your book.

If the title of your nonfiction book doesn't boldly promise to solve the readers' problem, you won't have a chance to sell them your book.

You need a working title early in your book-writing process, but you can change it as better ideas come to mind.

Famous book titles that were changed

Here are some examples of famous book titles that were changed before publication. Do you think the new titles are more intriguing?

- *Gone With the Wind* was first called *Tomorrow Is Another Day* (Margaret Mitchell)

- *To Kill a Mockingbird* was first called *Atticus* (Harper Lee)

- *Of Mice and Men* was first called *Something That Happened* (John Steinbeck)

- *War and Peace* was first called *All's Well That Ends Well* (Leo Tolstoy)

Do you think these famous books would have been as successful as they were if they had been published with the original titles?

Four tips to help you come up with a title

1. **It should be easy to remember.**

2. **Make your title short.** Short titles are the best, but longer titles can sometimes be more intriguing. You don't want to have so many words in your title that the words are too small to be easily read when someone is looking at Amazon's thumbnail image of your book. I like to keep my titles at seven words or less, but I sometimes exceed this limit.

3. **It needs to be original.** Search Amazon's books to see if there is already a book with your title. Also, Google your title and see what you can find out. It's not illegal if your book has the same title as another book, but it's easier to market your book if its title is unique.

4. **Make it intriguing.** This is important.

The four previous rules or tips are useful when deciding if the title you have come up with for your book is any good, but how do you come up with a title in the first place?

Techniques to find the best title for your novel

- **Sometimes, a good title will pop into your head.** If you're writing a nonfiction book, you know your topic well. If you're writing a novel, you know your characters and plot well, and your subconscious brain has a lot of material to work with. So, be open to considering any titles that pop into your head.

- **Do some research.** Take an important point in your plot or about your main character and do some research to see if you can come across a unique short phrase that would be a good title.

- **Don't use a one-word title.** If you have a two, three, or four-word phrase for your title, when someone searches Amazon or Google for the phrase, there's a good chance they will find your book, but if the title of your book is only one word, there's no way they will ever find it by searching for a single word. Plus, there's no way a single word can be an intriguing title.

- **Modify the best line in your story.** While you're writing or reading over your story, find a line you like. Then, modify it, shorten it, and maybe rearrange some words. See if you can come up with a title for your novel.

- **Have a title that's easy to say, remember, and spell.** You don't want to have a title that no one can remember or one that contains words that are hard to spell or pronounce. How can your readers recommend your book to their friends if they can't remember the title?

- **Come up with at least a dozen titles.** After you come up with several titles, go over your list, pick the title you like best, and use it as the working title of your book. Look over (and add to) your list from time to time while you're writing, and feel free to change your working title. I almost always make changes to my book's title while I'm writing the book.

Take a look at these suggested book titles for novels:

- *The Girls Are Gone*

- *27 Days on a Raft*

- *The First Lie Is Usually the Best*

- *Why Didn't I Tell Her?*

- *What Happened to Amy?*

Did any of these book title ideas make you want to read the book or at least take a closer look at it? Did any of these titles intrigue you? These are not titles of books. They are ideas to get you thinking.

Coming up with your book's title is an important task that will take time. Don't make the mistake of putting a lot of time into writing your book and then quickly giving it a lousy title.

The main takeaway from this chapter: Don't expect to be able to come up with your perfect title in one sitting. Coming up with a great title is a process. Follow the steps and ideas I've presented in this chapter, and eventually, you'll come up with a title you'll love.

Chapter 5
Your Book Needs an Eye-Catching Cover

"You can't judge a book by its cover, but you can sure sell a bunch of books if you have a good one."

~ Jayce O'Neal

More than 65% of all the books sold in the world (both printed books and eBooks) are sold by Amazon. I assume that's how you'll be selling your book, so you need a cover that will grab people's attention when they're browsing Amazon's books.

Amazon publishes more than 7,500 new books every day, so how can you get someone to notice your book?

An eye-catching cover will get your book noticed

Now that you have a working version of your title, you need to get your cover designed next.

To get your book noticed, you need a professional-looking and attention-grabbing cover. A boring, hard-to-read cover will not do the trick.

The sole purpose of your book cover is to get your book noticed. It's not the purpose of your cover to describe your book or tell what it's about. After someone notices your cover and clicks on your book, they'll be taken to Amazon's detail page and see your exciting and compelling description, telling them what the book is about and why they should read it.

Don't spend the long hours required to write your profound book and then not take the time and effort to have the cover designed that your book deserves. Your book deserves better than a wimpy-looking cover.

Think about this. When a potential buyer types a keyword phrase into the Amazon search box, Amazon shows a page of 20 small book cover images. Your book cover must stand out with the right font, color, and maybe a picture to grab someone's attention.

Having an eye-catching book cover designed before you start writing will also motivate you to keep writing your book.

Hire a professional to design your book cover

All you need to start with is the cover of your eBook to look at to keep you motivated, so get the eBook cover designed. You can get someone on Fiverr.com to design an eBook cover for $10. (Note that eBooks don't have a back cover.)

Most book covers are designed in layers, and changing the title or subtitle is easy. I often change the title or subtitle as I'm writing a book, and my designer usually doesn't charge me anything to make the change. Note that novels don't normally have a subtitle, but nonfiction books always need one.

I have designed my own book covers in the past, but I never do it now. Just because you know how to use Photoshop and can design your own cover, that doesn't mean you should. Designing an attention-grabbing book cover is a skill that even most graphic designers lack.

You can hire an expert book cover designer on Fiverr for $10 to $20. For my last half-dozen books, I've used Olivia on Fiverr.com. She is in Ukraine and will design a great eBook cover for $10.

You can't have the print version designed until you finish writing and formatting your book because you'll need the page count to know how thick to make the spine.

I usually know (or at least have an idea about) what photo or image I want to use, and sometimes I know what typeface and colors I want to use on my book cover, but not always. Sometimes, I'll give the designer more than one image and pay her to create several designs for me.

I used Fiverr.com and Olivia in Ukraine and paid her $40 to design four different front covers for this book. The one I chose is unconventional-looking and it's attention-getting. Remember, that's the purpose of a book cover—to catch someone's attention and get them to stop scrolling and take a look at your book.

I sometimes give designers a free hand and tell them to use their imagination to design my book cover, but most of the time, I have some idea about what I want my cover to look like. Many times, I'll spend the money to design more than one book cover and then choose the one I like the best.

What makes a great book cover?

- Remember, the job of your book cover is to grab readers' attention, not to describe your book.

- Some graphic designers want to use fancy fonts that are hard to read, and some of them don't like bright colors.

You don't want a washed-out-looking book cover.

- The title on the thumbnail version of your book cover that Amazon displays should be easy to read.

- Most nonfiction books have a subtitle, and most novels don't. If you have a subtitle, it's okay for it to be long and in smaller print.

- When you compare your book cover to books in your genre, which book would you buy?

- A bad cover will kill your book's chances of success. Your cover needs to look like it was designed by a professional.

After you have a professional design of a cover for your book, look at it closely to see how it compares to the points I've listed.

What goes on the back cover?

When looking at books in a bookstore, people often look at the back cover while holding the book in their hands. Even though Amazon shows an image you can click and see the back cover, most people never take the time to click on it and read what's on it. But a few will, so you'll need a back cover that will help sell your book.

- Start with an attention-getting opening headline followed by a sentence that describes your book.

- Then (if it's a nonfiction book), say something like, "Here's what you'll discover," followed by some bullet points.

- Also, if it's a nonfiction book, talk about the benefits to the readers and not the features. There's a difference. (A feature is the information in the book. A benefit is what it will do for the readers.)

- Include one or more quotes from your book or one of your best endorsements.

- If you have a website, be sure to include the URL.

- Near the bottom of the back cover, promote yourself. Include an "About the Author" paragraph along with your picture. Some writers don't want to put their picture on the back cover, but if readers feel like they know you, they're more likely to leave a review.

- This section should sound like someone else talking about you. In other words, it should be written in the third-person format.

Have your cover designed before you start writing

Here's an easy way to almost guarantee your book will get finished and published.

Before you write much, have a working version of your cover designed. Paste it at the top of your manuscript or on your wall, where you can see it every day.

Less than 0.6% of the books people start writing ever get finished because they lose interest and are no longer motivated to keep writing. Don't let this happen to you.

Having the cover of your book posted where you will see it daily will motivate you to finish it.

I don't know of anyone who hasn't finished writing and publishing their book when they've had a cover designed before they started writing it.

If you want to stack the deck in your favor and help ensure your book gets written and published, get busy and get a cover designed.

The main takeaway from this chapter: Conventional wisdom is often wrong and the old cliché that says people don't judge a book by its cover is dead wrong. Spend the time, effort, and money required to get a professional-looking, attention-grabbing cover. Don't settle for a so-so book cover. You will put a lot of time and effort into writing your book. Be sure to have the stunning, attention-grabbing cover that your book deserves—and get it designed before you do much writing.

Chapter 6
Everything Has to Happen Somewhere

"I write to discover what I know."

~ Flannery O'Connor

Your story needs a setting, which is where the action takes place. Since everything has to happen somewhere, you have to decide on a setting. You can choose a real or fictitious place, but be sure to describe it so your readers feel like they're there or have been there.

Your setting needs to be compelling. If your story takes place in an interesting location, you've already captured the readers' attention and have them excited before your story gets started.

If you're describing a real place, visit it if possible (even if you've been there many times before). Look at it as if you're seeing it for the first time. It will be easier to describe when you're standing there looking at it.

You may have to use your imagination if you're describing downtown London or the Amazon jungle.

While it's not as good as being there, looking at a picture while writing a description of a place will be helpful. You'll see things in the picture you wouldn't see in your imagination.

The setting is not just the physical location but also the mood and, in some cases, the time period.

Your setting doesn't have to be some exotic place—everything could happen at a kitchen table—but it's easier to write an intriguing story when the setting is interesting.

Describe the setting vividly in the early part of your story and it will help draw your readers into it. You want to take your readers out of their world and bring them into the world of your story.

If possible, you don't want your readers to realize you're describing the setting. Work your description into the story and add to it as the story progresses.

Why your setting is so important

You've nailed the characters and the plot. Is there anything else that's important for your book? You might think you have everything covered, but one big thing would be missing. What about the setting? Where is everything taking place? What is the mood? When is the story taking place?

The setting drives the story

Change the setting, and you'll change the story.

You could take the same characters with the same problems in your story now, place them downtown in New York City, in Nicaragua, or on the Appalachian Trail, and you would have a completely different story.

How do you describe a setting without being boring?

There is a fine line between too much and too little information. It's probably not important that the main character is wearing his blue shirt this morning, but maybe it is. It depends on the story.

When your character enters a new room, new town, or arrives on a new planet, you need to describe it so the readers can picture where the character is, but how much and what information should you include in your description? Many sensory details are necessary to describe a new setting fully, but how can you convey all of this without boring your readers?

To decide how much information is necessary for you to give to your readers and what's important, ask yourself these three questions:

- What's going on in this scene, and what is most relevant to the characters?

- What does the narrator want to draw the readers' attention to?

- What's different for the readers?

You could say your main character is in the Florida Everglades. But how much better would your story be if you said he was floating in the hot, sweltering Everglades with mosquitos buzzing all around his head and alligators nearby keeping an eye on him, waiting for him to fall out of the boat?

You want your reader to be in the boat with your main character, swatting the same mosquitos and experiencing the same feelings and concerns your character is feeling.

You want to describe the setting from the point of view of your main character. What's important to them? What do they see, hear, feel, and smell? If you have trouble doing this, picture yourself as the main character in the same situation. What would you see, feel, and think?

You'll probably have more than one setting

Parts of your story will likely take place in more than one setting. Some things may happen in the school parking lot, some downtown in a big city, and others on a farm in South Carolina.

Make sure your readers always have a picture in their minds of where the action is taking place. You want them to feel like they're right there observing what's going on.

Your setting could be a real place or a fictional place. It could be in South Georgia during a hot July summer, in the African jungle, or on the street you live on. Or maybe it's on a farm in Kentucky like the one your grandparents live on.

For some stories, when things are happening is important, and sometimes it's not. Is your story taking place in the spring of 2020, when schools were starting to be closed because of COVID-19, or in 1861, when the Civil War was about to start?

For some stories, the date is not important, but what's happening is. Maybe the story is taking place the week before the big game or on Monday after the prom.

You need to strike a balance between boring your readers with too much useless information and not telling them enough.

How to reveal the right amount of information about the setting

The key is to show what's important to the character (or what will be important later in the story). Knowing that the setting is important to the main character, think about what would be important to you if you were in the same situation. You always want to leave a lot about the setting to the readers' imagination. Fill in what's necessary, but let the readers fill in the rest.

Different scenes in your book can change the mood. There may be dangerous, enjoyable, or suspenseful times in all of these settings, and each will have a different mood.

Your descriptive words will help to set the mood. Choose these words carefully, and your readers will feel the mood.

A practice exercise

To practice what you've learned in this chapter about describing settings, take one scene from the story you're working on (or thinking about) and describe it in three different ways, using one sentence in each description.

1. In the first sentence, describe the context. How does the narrator feel about the setting?

2. In the second sentence, have the narrator draw the reader's attention to one thing about the new setting that's important or will be important later.

3. In the third sentence, have the narrator describe something that's different from what the readers were expecting.

You won't answer these three questions for every setting you describe, but thinking about them will help you start describing scenes in your book.

See there, writing settings is not so hard after all. You already know how to do it and are good at it.

The main takeaway from this chapter: Your story's setting (or settings) is super-important to your novel. For some stories, everything happens in one general area. However, changing settings occasionally can be useful to keep your readers interested and involved. Give a lot of thought to where your story is going to take place. Your settings and how you describe them can make your ordinary story outstanding.

Chapter 7
Who Is Telling the Story?

"The best time to plan a book is while you're doing the dishes."

~ Agatha Christie

Writers call the question of who is telling the story the story's point of view or POV. In other words, who is narrating the story?

Stories can be told in the first, second, or third person, and you can change between these in your story. However, this makes it harder to write and can confuse the reader unless done carefully and correctly.

First-Person Narration POV

One of the easiest ways to write a book is to have the main character tell the story in the first person. Make it easy on yourself and tell your story in the first person. Let the main character tell the story.

When the story is told from the main character's point of view (POV), it has the added advantage of helping the reader quickly feel like they know the main character.

Different POV Examples

Here's an example of first-person narration: "The first day, when he walked into English class, I had no way of knowing how he was going to change my life."

If it were told in the second person, the narrator would say, "She saw him walk into English class, and she had no idea how he was going to change her life."

If the story were being told from the main character's point of view but by someone else, it would be in the third person. Fantasy stories sometimes use this technique.

This is the hardest way to write a story. Since you're not trying to learn everything about writing novels right now but want to write your first book, forget all the options and write your story using the easy, first-person narrative technique.

If you have your main character tell the story from their point of view, it will be much easier to write, and the readers won't get lost or confused.

How a ball game can help you write your story

Imagine you're sitting in the bleachers waiting for the game to start, and a stranger sitting next to you is telling you a story about something that happened to them.

In the beginning, you don't know the person telling you the story, but as the story moves along, you get to know them, know more about them, and start to care more about them, which will make you care more about their story.

Keep the ball game concept in your head as you begin your story, and I think you'll find it much easier to get into writing it.

After all, you're just sitting at the ball game, listening to the main character tell you what happened. While you're hearing the voice in your head telling you the story, you're writing it down. What could be easier?

Hear the main character in your head

Even though you're creating a fictional person, you need to get to know them well, just like they were real.

If you're basing your main character loosely on a real person you know, spend some time listening to them talk. Listen carefully and pick up on their tone and phrasing. Are they usually funny, sarcastic, or excited? Do they talk fast or slow? Do they ramble a lot or get to the point quickly? Do they usually speak in long sentences or short ones? Or do they even speak in complete sentences?

If listening to them in person is impossible, try calling them and just chatting. Long conversations are best if you both have the time. The longer you talk, the more you'll get to know the person. What they say is not important—it's how they say it. As a last resort, try recalling times you've heard them talking. Try to hear their voice in your head.

Become your character

When you're writing your manuscript, you want to become the character doing the narration. The more you develop the character and get to know them, the easier this will become. If you become Huck Finn on the raft floating down the Mississippi

River, it will be a lot easier for you to tell the story. Maybe that's what Mark Twain did when he wrote the story.

In the beginning, the voice you hear in your head may sound a lot like your own, but as your character develops and the more you get into the narration, the more you will become the character. If the character has an accent, you may even start to hear the accent in your head.

Your story will get easier to write the more you get to know and become the character you're creating. Your goal should be to get inside the heads of each of your characters and know how they think and act in different situations. The more you can become your character when writing your book, the better your story will be.

Since you don't have an outline, let the main character tell you the story. You never know where they may take you or what direction your story may go.

The main takeaway from this chapter: You have to decide who will tell your story before you can start writing. You have several options, but writing your story in the first person from the point of view of the main character will make your story come together easier and quicker, and it will be easier to write.

Chapter 8
Bring Your Characters to Life

"When I used to teach writing, I would tell the students to make their characters want something right away."

~ Kurt Vonnegut

Characters are the lifeblood of your story. You need a story-worthy character for your hero or main character. And you need a few other realistic, interesting, and believable characters.

One of the biggest challenges you will face when writing your novel is creating a main character that readers can connect with.

Early in your book, you want your readers to identify with the hero and begin to cheer for him in your story. You also need to let the readers know what the hero desires and dreads the most. What does he want more than anything else and what is he most afraid of? Maybe a sense of impending doom or disaster.

Bringing your main character to life at the beginning of a story (maybe even in the first sentence) is a great way to pull your readers in immediately.

Here are some examples:

"I thought going to an all-girls school was going to eliminate most of my problems instead of creating way more than I had before."

"We pulled out of the driveway, and I was excited to finally be going to the beach for the first time."

"I had spent my whole life living on our farm, and I wasn't sure I was going to like living in a big city."

Try seamlessly blending your character's physical and emotional description and personality into the story. This is much better than just stopping your story and writing a paragraph or so describing your character.

When you can describe your characters while keeping the story moving along, readers will start to know and connect with them without even knowing they're doing it.

Never show a picture of any of your characters

You want to provide some information and a description of your characters, but not too much. For example, you never want to show a picture of any of the characters. Let the readers' imagination fill in the details. You can say she is beautiful, has long red hair, and is in her mid-30s. You can say she likes pizza and chocolate cake and loves country music but hates jazz. Let your readers picture the characters in their minds.

Take the time to write several intriguing and compelling openings

You can do this before you even know the plot or anything about the story you're going to write. Keep writing these openings. You may be surprised when a plot or story idea pops into your head. Write at least a dozen or more over a few days. Don't expect to get magical results in one sitting.

More proof that conventional wisdom is often wrong

Most beginning writers try to come up with a story idea or plot and then pull their hair out, trying to come up with a killer (or even a good) opening line. But you can go against the grain and do things backward—at least, that's what a lot of people will think about the technique I've just described.

What I've described is one more of the many ways you'll find where conventional wisdom is wrong. In this book, I'll continue to show you that it's often wrong and how you can use this new technique to your advantage. You'll find the concept especially helpful when you're writing your story.

Let everyone else wonder how you came up with your story, characters, and their interesting misadventures. You won't have to tell them that you went against conventional wisdom in your thinking and storytelling techniques.

Characters are the secret sauce for your story

The characters you come up with and develop will turn an ordinary, dull story into a compelling and memorable story.

Take the time to create interesting and intriguing characters that your readers will love, admire, or want to know more about.

Your story will be easier to write when you have characters that your readers will be fond of or intrigued by, so make it easy on yourself and write your story this way. Readers like to fall in love with a hero.

Is the main character someone they can identify with? Do they love him, feel sorry for him, or want to be like him? You definitely want your readers to want to know what the main character will do next and what will happen to him.

Would you want the main character to be your boyfriend, girlfriend, husband, wife, best friend, or roommate? You want to have a main character your readers would like to spend time with.

You want to create characters that are interesting. Maybe you can use a modified version of people you know. If you do this, make the character different enough from the real person so no one recognizes them.

One of the best ways to create a character is to let it be a mixture of more than one person. Take traits of different people you know and create a character. You could do this for all your characters.

You'll need more than one character, and they will all need to be different.

The advantage of basing characters on people you know is that it will be easier for you to describe their traits, actions, and looks. Of course, you'll want to modify their looks—hair color, age, name, etc.

Bake some characters from scratch

It's also helpful to create one or more characters totally from scratch. Come up with the characteristics you want your character to have. This is an especially good way to create your main character.

For example, is he or she honest, strong, weak, smart, silly, witty, ambitious, devious, lazy, hard-working, athletic, good-looking, beautiful, etc.?

You'll need a strong, vivid, interesting character as your main character to keep your readers interested and keep them reading and involved in your story.

You need to get to know your characters well. Have a page for each character with everything you know about them written on it. You don't need to use everything you know about a character in your story. But when you know your characters well, you'll be able to predict what they would say and how they would act in a certain situation.

Here are some things you need to know about your characters

Start with what you know now and add to each character's sheet as you learn more about them.

Knowing a lot about each character will make it easier for you to write your story. It helps you know what each character would do or say in a situation. When you instinctively know what they would say or do in a situation, you'll know that you fully understand your characters and your writing will be easier.

- What does your character want more than anything else?

This could have a lot to do with your story.

- If the character is a female, does she have a boyfriend or a husband? Is she married? Does she have any kids? Does she have a dog or a cat, and if so, what kind?

- If the character is a male, does he have a girlfriend or a wife?

- Describe their family.

- If they have a job, what do they do? How did they get the job? Are they looking to change jobs?

- Are they retired?

- How old is your character? You may not reveal their exact age, but knowing their age can help you predict how they would act in any given situation.

- Have they been in the military?

- What has happened in their life that they are still dealing with?

- Where do they live, and have they always lived there? Do they want to move somewhere else, and if so, where and why?

- Do they have a car, boat, or motorcycle? If so, describe it.

- Are they still in school, or have they graduated? Are they planning to go back to school?

- What are their plans for the future?

- What are they most afraid of or afraid will happen (or not happen)?

- What is the one thing they have done that they don't want anybody to know about?

Your characters don't have to be fully developed before you start writing your story. They can grow and change, and more can be revealed about them as the story progresses. If your characters change as the story progresses, make sure nothing changes about them that contradicts anything that has been said or revealed earlier in the book. If it does, go back and change what needs to be updated.

For example, if a character has long black hair in the beginning, but then you want them to be a feisty redhead, you can do that, but you'll have to go back and make sure they have red hair from the beginning.

Your characters can grow and change but can't contradict a previous trait.

Most of your characters will need to have a name

Here are some important things to remember about the names of your characters:

The names of each of your characters should start with a different letter. You don't want John, James, Jill, and Jenny to be your characters.

If you use first and last names, they should not both be long. You can have Bill Livingston or Anthony Fox, but you don't want to have Anthony Livingston.

Use easy-to-pronounce names. Many people will sound out the names in their heads as they read your book.

It's okay to use a nickname. Sometimes, a nickname can help describe a character. For example, what comes to mind when you hear the following nicknames?

Big John, Sneaky, Barbie, Rambo, Tank, Shorty, Goofball, Amigo, Baby Girl, Chief, Cupcake, Giggles, and Boss Man. These nicknames help give your readers a picture of the character.

The main takeaway from this chapter: Developing unique and interesting characters your readers can identify with, get to know, and understand is one of the most important parts of writing a good book. If your readers don't like your main character, they will find it hard to like your book.

Chapter 9

How to Start Writing Your Book

"The scariest moment is always just before you start."

~ Stephen King

If you sit down and stare at a blank page, you may have trouble deciding what to write or even how to begin.

One fail-safe place to start your story is when the main character starts something new. Is your main character going on a trip, starting a new relationship, moving to a new town, getting divorced, attending the first day at a new school, or starting a new job? These situations are all interesting ways to start a story because something is about to happen.

Starting anything new involves strong emotions and the feeling of realizing "anything can happen." You want your readers to feel this same excitement, anxiety, and adrenaline rush. This will quickly pull them into the story.

You can start a story in the middle or even at the end and then do flashbacks, but when you do that, the story is harder to write and more difficult to pull the reader into, so why make things harder for yourself? Start your story at the beginning.

That doesn't mean you have to start writing your story at the beginning. You can start writing at the point you're most passionate about and come back and write the beginning later.

Reveal information in a natural way

You want your readers to know a lot about the characters, the setting, and what has happened to bring them to this point, but they don't need to know all of this at once. You can weave this information into your story as it moves along and do it in a natural way.

You want a strong opening and vivid characters that will keep your readers turning pages. If they do this, they will find out all this information as your story progresses.

In most stories, the main character desperately wants something or wants something to happen, but as you might expect, there are roadblocks. Reveal this information early to pull the readers into the story.

One problem with starting a story is that you have too many options. You're free to say anything you want.

Sidney Sheldon made this point clearly when he said, "A blank piece of paper is God's way of telling us how hard it is to be God."

3 things are important to have a successful book

1. **You want your story to be easy to read.** Don't use words your target readers won't understand. Don't expect your readers to look up words they don't know. It won't happen.

2. **You want your book to be easy to understand.** If readers don't understand what you're trying to say or they get lost or confused, they'll likely put your book down and never pick it up again. They're reading your novel

for entertainment. And if they don't know what you're saying, they won't be entertained. You'll lose them in a heartbeat. If your story is jumping around too much with too many flashbacks and too many characters, it could be easy for a reader to get confused. A confused reader will stop reading your book.

3. **You want your book to be easy to remember.** Your readers are not likely to read your book in one sitting. After reading a few chapters, it might be two or three days before they get back to it. Can they still remember the different characters without getting them mixed up? Can they remember what's going on?

Are you going to write a novel or a nonfiction book?

This is the first thing you will have to decide before you can start writing your book. There are pros and cons to writing each type of book.

A nonfiction book is easier and faster to write, but writing a novel could be more fun. You will get to use your creativity and imagination when writing a novel, but a novel will be harder to write.

In addition to learning how to tell a story in your novel, you'll need to develop your plot, write and punctuate dialogue, develop characters, and describe places. It's not easy to be a good storyteller—but it can be profitable.

People search for novels by category (Romance, Drama, Science Fiction, Westerns, etc.) and not so much by keywords.

A novel and a nonfiction book are totally different animals

People buy a nonfiction book (also called a how-to book) to solve a problem or tell them how to do something.

In a nonfiction book, the title and subtitle have to make a clear and bold promise to solve a problem. And, of course, your nonfiction book must deliver on that promise.

It's easier to market a nonfiction book than a novel because people find nonfiction books by searching for keywords that describe their problem. When you have these keywords and phrases in your title, subtitle, or one of Amazon's seven keyword slots, people can find (and buy) your book.

When you write a nonfiction book, you combine your knowledge, experience, and research. It may be 90% knowledge and experience and 10% research or vice versa. It doesn't matter. The reader won't care where the information came from as long as it's there.

You might think you don't have much knowledge and experience in any topic that would qualify you to write a nonfiction book, at least not one that anyone would be interested in reading, but your knowledge and insights into a lot of topics are probably more interesting and valuable than you realize.

Another way to decide what topic to write a nonfiction book about is to think about what kind of book you would like to read. Then, do the research necessary to become an expert on that topic and write your book.

Research could be a big part of the fun of writing your book. Interviewing experts in the field could also be interesting and enjoyable. Most of them would be happy to talk to you when you tell them you're writing a book about the topic and would like to have their opinions on the subject.

Writing a novel can be fun

Even though a nonfiction book is easier and faster to write, many people dream of writing a novel. Writing a novel will likely be more enjoyable, and you'll get to use your imagination.

You'll need to learn a few things to help you write a great novel. I'll be covering those in the next few chapters. Then, in Chapter 17, I'll tell you more about how to write a nonfiction book.

When writers sit down to write a novel, sometimes one of the hardest things for them to do is to get started. In the next chapter, I'll discuss what I call story starters. In other words, how do you get your story started?

It would be a sin to start your story with a whimper

To write a good story, you must quickly pull the reader into it. Here are the four things a great story needs:

1. **An interesting place:** Everything has to happen somewhere. It could happen in China, in the living room, or in a Michigan lakehouse. The more interesting the place, the easier it is to pull the reader into your story.

2. **An intriguing main character or hero:** You can help make them intriguing by revealing their main desire and biggest dread.

3. **A riveting plot:** A little dog chewing on a bone is not riveting, but a little dog chewing on a bone that belongs to the big dog next door is riveting. Something is about to happen.

4. **Compelling prose:** Startle the reader from the very beginning. This is not easy, but give it your best effort and see if you can make it happen. Include some memorable lines when you can.

Many novels lack memorable lines, but if you can come up with one or more, your novel will be better than most others.

Here are some examples of openings that will startle the reader:

- Shortly after take-off, the left engine sputtered and died.

- I heard the sound of two gunshots coming from behind the cabin, but I didn't know what had happened. Was Sarah alright?

- Billy said, "I never want to see you again," and stormed out the door.

- Jenny was happy that she had landed her first full-time job until she walked into work the first day and saw who else was working there.

Do you need an outline?

Stephen King and several other great writers don't use an outline. They write from the seat of their pants, so to speak. They let the characters dictate what happens next.

They sometimes have a rough idea of what's going to happen: The detective will find out who did it, the guy will finally get the girl, etc.

Other writers work from a detailed outline. Start writing your novel without an outline and see where it goes. You might decide later that you need a rough outline for some scenes but not for the whole book.

Let the main character decide where the story goes. If the writer is surprised by what happens next, their readers will be surprised, too.

After you try writing without an outline, if you decide you could do a better job working from one, come up with an outline and see how that works. Your goal is to write your book. Do whatever works for you.

You need to write a gripping, good story

Whether you like it or not, writing a great novel isn't about descriptions, settings, or dialog—it's about *storytelling*. Descriptions, settings, and dialog are just the tools you use to help you tell your story.

Remember, you don't have to start writing at the beginning of your story. Start by writing the part you're most passionate about. Go back and write the beginning later.

Here's the main takeaway from this chapter: As Stephen King said in the quote at the beginning of the chapter, *"The scariest moment is always just before you start."* Getting started is also the most difficult. You can sit and look at a blank page for hours, waiting for the words to come. The simple solution is not to worry about what you're writing when you begin. Just start putting words on the page. Later, you'll probably go back and delete some (and maybe all) of your first few sentences anyway.

Chapter 10

Story Starters and Prompts for Novels

"The first draft is just you telling yourself the story."

~ Terry Pratchett

What kind of novel are you going to write? In this chapter, I'll discuss several basic categories.

You need an idea before you can start writing your story. But where can you find story ideas?

They're everywhere. You may find a story idea on the bottom shelf of aisle three in sporting goods at Walmart, or you might find an idea when you're staring out the window while sitting in the back of Mrs. Goldman's English class.

I've included some "story starter" openings for different categories in this chapter. You can start your story with one of these lines or a variation of one of these opening lines and then continue your story from there.

You can use these as the beginning of your novel or as the beginning of a chapter.

Your goal is to start writing

Benjamin Franklin said, "Either write something worth reading or do something worth writing."

You may think you haven't done anything worth writing about. Don't worry. You don't have to have done something worth writing about, but your main character does.

A famous writing friend of mine told me that the purpose of the first sentence is to get the readers to read the second sentence, and the purpose of the second sentence is to get them to read the third sentence. That may be an oversimplification, but there's a lot of wisdom in what he said.

It's easy for readers to put a book down, so you have to keep them interested and intrigued and build suspense.

Even though the first sentence is important, it's crucial not to get hung up on trying to create the perfect opening sentence for your story.

The important thing is to start telling your story. Keep in mind that, later, you may delete your first sentence, first paragraph, or even the first several pages. That's called editing. Your goal now is to get words on the page.

How to use these story starters

1. Scroll down to the genre that fits the kind of story you want to write.

2. Read over the story starter examples for that genre and find one that intrigues you.

3. Use the sample story starter (or your modified version of it) as your first line, and you'll be in business—you've started writing your novel.

4. Then, decide what happens next and what happens after that and keep writing. The most important thing is to

keep writing. Don't worry about whether what you're writing is good or bad. Most likely, it's bad, maybe even really bad, but you can fix that later. Your job now is to write.

5. Remember the quote at the beginning of this chapter: "The first draft is just you telling yourself the story." After you've told yourself the story, you can tweak it, put things in the proper order, tell it better, and edit it. Nora Roberts said, "You can fix anything except a blank page."

The important thing is to start writing and let the words flow. Don't even think about editing or rewriting. Just put words on the page.

Sometimes, that's easier said than done. I'll give you some sample opening sentences for different categories of novels. You're free to use them as they are, but in most cases, you'll need to modify them to better suit your story.

There are several genres to choose from. Below are a few of the more popular ones.

To be a good writer, you must read a lot. Read books by authors you like. One advantage of doing this is that your writing will start to sound like the author you like. It's also important for you to read books in your genre by other authors.

Start writing and make your story as unique as you are.

Story starters for different genres

Start by looking at the suggested opening lines for your genre, but if you need more ideas, take a look at the opening lines for other genres.

Romance

- I found out he was in my history class on the first day of the school year.

- This year is going to be different. I won't be timid. I'll take chances, and I will find true love.

- I saw her in the cafeteria and wondered who this new girl was. I felt I had to meet her, and that was my first mistake.

- The prom was in two weeks, and I didn't have a date. If I had asked someone, I would probably have had better luck, but that takes nerve.

- I never imagined what was in store for me when I came out of my shell.

- Everyone told me she would cause me trouble, but I never realized how much trouble she would cause.

- The only seat in class was next to the new girl, the most beautiful girl I had ever seen. Where did she come from? Did she have a boyfriend?

Science fiction

- When I saw a genetically modified girl for the first time, I couldn't believe my eyes.

- I started out working on this for a school project, and that's when strange things started happening.

- Three aliens were standing there looking at me. I wish I knew what they were thinking.

- When the opportunity to volunteer to travel to a nearby galaxy came up, I jumped at the chance, but I never expected this.

- The strange creature handed me a green stone and told me to always hold on to it. That's when my life started to change.

Mystery and crime

- I didn't know who to tell when I came across the new evidence.

- When I found the gun in the barn, I knew everyone had it all wrong.

- Most people thought it was an accident, but I knew what really happened.

- Sarah had been missing for three days. Everyone thought I had something to do with her disappearance.

- I was telling the truth, but the detectives wouldn't believe me.

Humor

Good humor is hard to write, even for experienced writers. If you like humor, you should include a little in your book. A little subtle humor will add a lot to your book, but trying to make your whole book funny won't be easy.

- Everything was going as planned until the chicken got loose.

- I was excited to finally land a summer job, but then I

found out what I would be doing.

- I thought it would be a fun senior prank, but little did I know what was about to happen.

- On the way to school this morning, I sat alone on the bus. How could anything go wrong?

- She didn't tell me the whole story. Girls usually don't.

- My boss is usually a pretty serious person, so when she called me into her office, I wasn't expecting what she said next.

- No one expected the squirrel to get out of the box.

Westerns

Writing a Western novel could be easy. The plots are usually straightforward and easy to follow. It's a good genre to choose if you enjoy it. You can watch some Western movies on YouTube or Netflix or read some Western novels and get a lot of ideas.

Below are some story starter lines to help get you going.

- The wagon train was going to head out first thing in the morning, and I couldn't wait.

- I had hopes of finding gold, but I knew there would be danger and no guarantee of ever finding any gold.

- Pa said we might go to town on Saturday. I had my hopes up.

- The West was not a safe place for a woman, but I was not going to be intimidated.

- Since the railroad came to town, everything has changed.

- I had thought about going back east, but Texas is my home. Raising cattle is all I know how to do.

Historical fiction

When writing historical fiction, it's important to keep the characters, setting, language, and a lot of other things working together. You'll probably need to do a lot of research and read some books set in the time period. Writing a historical novel can be a fun adventure if your heart's in it, but don't tackle this project lightly.

Here are some openings and story starter lines to get you going:

- I arrived in America excited and scared.

- Traveling to Italy was not what I expected.

- I had everything I owned in one bag when I boarded the steamship.

- If I was ever going to get away from home, now was the time to do it.

- The soldiers would start arriving any day, and there would be a lot of them.

- I had a new job as a telegraph operator, and my life in the big city was going to be exciting.

Children's books

Writing children's books is a whole different ball game. I have friends who do it, and they love it. There is much to learn to write children's books. In addition to writing, you will need illustrations. If you need help in this area, you can hire designers from Fiverr.com to do your graphics at a reasonable cost.

Start your story with a bang

Don't try to ease into your story. You should hit the ground running with things happening almost immediately.

You need to have a conflict or tension point in the first few pages. It doesn't have to be big, and it doesn't have to be the main conflict of the book. It will help show how the main character thinks and acts, help readers get to know the main character, and pull them into the story.

I can be creative and productive when I write while sitting in a coffee shop or early in the morning when I'm alone. It's good to get away from the house and write in a new environment sometimes. I find it especially helpful when I'm starting a story.

You don't want to start with pages and pages describing the setting with nothing happening. Your readers must connect with your main character in the opening pages.

Even experienced writers find flashbacks challenging. My advice is to tell your story in a linear fashion without using flashbacks.

You have to build some suspense in the first chapter of your book. Every book needs some suspense to keep the reader involved. You want to give them something to look forward to and make them want to continue reading the rest of the book.

The main takeaway from this chapter: The most important thing is to get started putting words on the page. You can rewrite and edit your work later. Don't waste valuable writing time fretting over trying to come up with the perfect opening line. After you've written several pages, you may be able to go back and find a profound thought for your opening. If you don't find a sentence you like, don't worry—it will come to you later. The key is to get busy putting words on the page.

Chapter 11
All Stories Need Some Suspense

"Sometimes I write better than I can."

~ Ernest Hemingway

Suspense is necessary to keep your readers turning pages.

You need a few subplots in your story. Things that happen in subplots create extra suspense.

Suspense is the unknown and anticipation your readers feel while waiting for something that's about to happen—or at least something they think is about to happen. It makes your readers concerned about what's going to happen to your character. Is he or she going to be okay?

Three things are necessary to create suspense

1. **You have to have a looming disaster.** It doesn't have to be life-threatening. For example, in your character's world, a looming disaster could be not getting a date for the prom.

2. **Make the readers wait for the event.** This causes anticipation and heightens the suspense.

3. **Suspense has to have a clear ending.** Let the event happen and tell what happened.

Suspense is usually a short event, but it can drag out over a few chapters or the whole book, but this is harder to pull off. If you have what is called long-term suspense, the conclusion has to be something big and satisfying. You can't deliver some so-so outcome after making your reader wait a long time.

It's better to have multiple short-term suspense events. It's a brief time of heightened anxiety. Short-term suspense usually lasts for one chapter or less.

There is also suspense when something is about to happen, but it doesn't have to be something bad. It could be something funny or romantic.

How to build suspense

To build suspense, you need to have your readers invested in the outcome and craving an answer. You can help make this happen by leaving clues that the readers won't recognize as a clue at the time but will recognize after the event happens. Then they will think, *Why didn't I see that coming?*

When you resolve a suspenseful situation, you don't want the outcome to be predictable. You want a believable but unexpected resolution.

The classic and easiest way to create suspense is to put a character the readers care about in danger. This technique can't be used in the early part of the book. It must be used after readers are invested in and care about the character. The more your readers care about a character, the easier it is to create suspenseful situations.

Long-term and short-term suspense

You need both long-term and short-term suspense, and you can have them at the same time. In a murder mystery, for example, there could be long-term suspense where the main character is accused of murder, and it takes the whole book to resolve that he didn't do it. At the same time, several short-term suspenseful situations could take place.

It's also important that the character doesn't have an easy and obvious way out of the situation. The situation needs to look hopeless to be suspenseful, and you don't want the reader to see the resolution coming.

At times, you want the suspense to be so intense that your readers will forget about other things they should be doing.

You must first create characters your readers care about before they'll be concerned about what happens to them.

The more your readers feel like they know a character, their thoughts, goals, fears, desires, concerns, and worries, the more they'll care about what happens to them.

Different types of suspense

All suspense doesn't have to involve something dangerous or life-threatening about to happen to your beloved character. Suspense can be about whether the football team captain will ask Jill to the prom when he sees her this afternoon.

After all, he did tell her when he hurried past her as she came out of history class that he wanted to ask her something this afternoon after school.

Slowing things down can build suspense

You want to make your readers wait while the tension builds, so don't move things along too fast.

One way to slow things down and build suspense is to use short sentences. Mixing in a few one- or two-word sentences will do the trick.

The words you use to describe what's happening, the sounds, and what the characters are thinking can all help build suspense. To build extra suspense, you may want to use a few more adjectives than you normally use.

Mark Twain said, "When you catch an adjective, kill it."

Maybe he didn't mean to kill all adjectives because he didn't kill all of his adjectives. He used some, but he used them sparingly. When you don't use many adjectives, the ones you do use are powerful.

You can also heighten suspense by dropping clues in earlier paragraphs.

You can say things such as there has been an increase in crime lately, especially after dark. You can add that Ashley has been hearing strange sounds outside her house lately. And now that the power has gone off, she is starting to get scared.

You can throw in the clue that her cell phone battery has died in an earlier paragraph. It wasn't important when you mentioned the dead battery, but now it's becoming important. Her cell phone battery is dead, and she doesn't have a way to charge it. Nothing has happened yet, but suspense and tension are building.

Don't give up on your book

After you've worked on your novel for a while, you may get tired of it or start to become bored with it and start thinking it's not as good as you thought it was in the beginning.

Stephen King's wife, Tabitha, found the manuscript of his first novel in the trash. She got it out, read it, and convinced him to publish it. That book is still selling well 50 years later. He had worked on it so long that he was convinced it wasn't any good and that it belonged in the trash.

It's easy to get discouraged and start thinking your novel isn't any good. It's easy to be excited about your fantastic opening and the killer ending you are eager to start writing (at least, you were at one time), but you can get discouraged and bored and let your book die in the middle.

Suspense keeps you and the reader interested in the story. If you don't keep the readers excited and engaged in the middle, they'll never see your surprise ending.

If you become bored with your book, you can be sure your readers will be bored. The worst thing a writer can do is bore their readers. You can never have a good book without a good middle.

Here is a general outline for your story. Follow this formula, and you won't have any trouble deciding what to write next.

- What does the main character need or want?

- What stands in the way of him getting what he wants?

- What is he trying to do about it?

- Everything he tries to do to fix the problem only makes things worse until all appears hopeless.

- Conclude the story with an unexpected resolution and your unique ending.

That's the main plot (or outline) of your story.

The main takeaway from this chapter: Suspense is not just for mystery-type novels. All stories (horror, comedy, romance, etc.) need some suspenseful events to keep the reader interested and wanting to know what's going to happen next. You create suspense anytime you have the reader waiting for an answer or resolution. Don't overuse this tool, but be sure to include just the right mixture of suspense in your story to keep the reader turning the pages.

Chapter 12
How to Write Engaging Descriptions

"Everything that needs to be said has already been said. But, since no one was listening, everything must be said again."

~ André Gide

Writing vivid and engaging descriptions can be challenging. It's also difficult to know what to include and what to leave out.

When you write descriptions correctly, you can make people, places, and things come to life.

You must describe your characters, the setting, and everything else that's important in your story, but you shouldn't do it all at once. That would bore your readers.

Your writing style doesn't matter

When you describe people, settings, and things, you may wonder if you're being overly dramatic or fancy or too simple and bland. What is your writing style? The simple answer is that it doesn't matter.

You're not describing anything. Your character is. How would they describe things? When you tell your story from the main character's point of view, it's their voice that describes it. The more you can become your character the easier it will be to tell their story.

Try to hear their voice in your head when you're writing. Do they have an accent? They probably do if they're from Boston, London, Louisiana, Australia, South Africa, or South Alabama. Can you hear their accent in your head? Be careful using their accent in your writing. It could backfire if you're not good at it, but try to hear and use the words they would use.

Work your descriptions into the dialogue when possible

When you can do that, the readers may not even realize you're describing things. Also, when you can weave descriptions into the dialogue, it can often reveal a lot about the characters.

Mixing your description in with the dialogue will keep the story moving. The reader may see the setting in his mind and not even realize that you've described it to him.

Make sure your readers can picture where the action is taking place. Make them feel like they're in the picture. A good description is always clear.

When describing things, keep it simple. You don't need to describe everything. Describe the things that are important to the story—or will become important later.

Don't describe something just so that you can get on with the story. When possible, make your description an integral part of your story.

How your character sees and describes the world can tell the reader a lot about the character and what is being described. Use this to your advantage.

A good description of your characters and settings will help bring the characters to life and make the settings seem real.

How to make your descriptions interesting and more original

Use words that describe things the reader can see. Don't use abstract words that your readers can't picture. Words such as loss, happiness, sadness, grief, and peace are not descriptive.

Use strong nouns and verbs. Instead of saying he put on his shoes, say he put on his black alligator cowboy boots. When you describe something, you want the readers to picture it in their minds.

Give specific details. Don't be vague. Instead of saying he was changing the tire on his car, you could say he was changing the tire on his prized antique 1932 black A Model Ford, his white 1965 Corvette, or his 2018 gas-saving Prius. The readers can picture these cars. This description also tells the readers more about the character, what he likes, and what he's interested in.

When you describe your character taking a walk in the evening, does he enjoy the vast array of twinkling stars or complain about the mosquitos and the hot, muggy air? Each of these descriptions tells the readers something different about the character.

Add some descriptions of things moving. This makes the setting come to life. For example, a fly buzzing around the table, the curtains flapping in the wind, or the dog jumping upon the sofa.

Use powerful descriptive words

You don't want to use words your readers don't know the meaning of, but using words they know but don't use often works wonders in your descriptions.

Here are 13 of my favorite underused descriptive words:

- Roaring—when describing a river

- Thud—as in a loud thud

- Rumbling

- Filthy

- Savory

- Toxic

- Hazy

- Uncanny

- Pungent

- Musty

- Dilapidated

- Cuddly

Do you see how these words would cause the reader to see a picture or experience a feeling, smell, or taste?

Where and when is the story taking place?

If it's important to your story, readers will want to know where and when your story is taking place.

If your story is set in the current time, that will be obvious, but if it takes place in 1861, just before the start of the Civil War, during Shakespeare's time, in the spring of 2020, when schools were starting to shut down because of the COVID-19 pandemic, or in the future in the year 3,010, you need to make that clear.

With the right choice of words, you can tell your readers a lot in one sentence. You want them to picture the scene and what you're describing, but don't drag it out.

How to describe emotions

In general, people try to hide most of their emotions when they're in public, so to make your character seem real, don't overdo their expressions of emotion. You can describe some emotions when the situation calls for it.

When you describe your character's emotions or reactions to a situation, think about how he or she would act. You want your character to come across as a real person. They can have quirks and their own personality but don't make them act melodramatic when that's not their nature.

Three final points about writing descriptions

#1. Take your time and write good, compelling descriptions of your characters. Their actions will be much stronger when you've described them well. When you're describing characters, your goal should be to help your readers feel like they know them. Your description should be more than just a physical description. It should also include things such as their goals and ambitions, what they're afraid of or worried about, and what they're thinking and feeling.

#2. Provide vivid descriptions of settings. Your readers need to be able to see where things are taking place, whether at the beach, on the front porch, in the living room, or downtown in a real or fictional town. Even if you're describing the town or a section of the town where you live now or where you used to live, you can do a much better job of describing it if you visit it again and look at it like you're seeing it for the first time. You can better describe a setting for your readers if you visit it again with the sole purpose of describing it.

#3. If you're describing a fictional place, visit a similar place if possible. Pretend it's the place where your story is taking place and describe it. Don't rely totally on your imagination when you're trying to see and describe a setting if you don't have to. Sprinkle a few adjectives into your descriptions, but don't overdo it. A little goes a long way, like using salt, pepper, and spices when you're cooking. Of course, if your story is taking place in the Amazon jungle, the Sahara Desert, or downtown London, it might not be feasible for you to visit.

The main takeaway from this chapter: How well you can describe characters, settings, and scenes will have a lot to do with how much your readers will enjoy your book. You want them to feel like they're standing in the middle of the story or observing it from close by. You want them to get this feeling without realizing you're describing things for them.

Chapter 13

How to Write Compelling Dialogue

"We cannot direct the wind, but we can adjust the sails."

~ Dolly Parton

Everybody will tell you that dialogue is important, but what is dialogue anyway?

In your novel, it's when two people talk with a purpose or agenda.

In real life, two people are often "shooting the breeze" with no agenda, but that's not the case in a novel.

Real-world speech meanders, but the dialogue in your novel should never wander aimlessly. It should come from a character with a purpose and an agenda and be directed to another character with a different agenda.

This is a key point to remember when you're writing dialogue.

It's important to know each person's purpose or agenda before you start writing that section of dialogue.

Writing dialogue can be fun

Having great dialogue in your novel can turn an ordinary novel into a captivating and enticing one. Enhancing the dialogue is the fastest, easiest, and best way to improve any novel.

The best part is that writing dialogue is the most fun part of writing your novel. You get to use your creativity and imagination to bring your story to life.

Sometimes, dialogue consists of only one word, and that word can be more powerful than a long sentence. For example, when one person asks, "Does your wife know about this?" and the other responds, "Maybe," that one word says more than any long sentence could ever convey. That one word intrigues the reader to want to know more.

Dialogue can reveal what a character is thinking. A comment can be made and then followed by "she thought" instead of "she said."

Dialogue can be informational or conflictual. It can also reveal the speaker's mood: Are they angry, sad, or worried?

Dialogue can be used for character development, to provide information, or to describe feelings. It can reveal so much, making your story much more interesting than when you use narration to tell the reader everything.

You can use indirect dialogue in your book, such as, "I found out yesterday why he didn't tell me the truth."

Make your dialogue powerful and intriguing

Great dialogue should give the reader the sense they're eavesdropping. You don't ever want your dialogue to sound artificial.

To write good dialogue, pay attention to the conversations you hear when walking down the hall at school. Listen to conversations when you're in McDonald's or hanging out at a ball game with your friends. It doesn't matter what the topic is. Listen to the way people talk.

An even better technique is to put a cell phone or recorder in your pocket and record conversations. Then, go home and transcribe those conversations. Pay attention to how often they cut each other off, change the subject, use "uh," etc. Work these quirks into the dialogue you write, and it will sound real.

If your dialogue is boring or doesn't sound natural, it will destroy even the best story. If you write your dialogue well, it will grab the reader and pull them into the story. You need compelling, correctly punctuated dialogue to have an intriguing story.

Dialogue allows your reader to get to know the characters better and learn what's going on in their lives.

How to write dialogue tags

Dialogue tags tell readers who is talking, but they should not be overused. That will distract from what is being said.

One way to accomplish this is by using dialogue tags your readers don't even notice. About 80% of the time, you should simply use "she said" and "he asked." Readers see these words so often their conscious minds won't realize they saw them.

Don't try to get fancy with tags. This will distract the reader. Occasionally, if you need to describe volume, you can use words such as "whispered," "shouted," or "yelled," but use these sparingly.

You can place the tag before, after, or in the middle of your dialogue. Mix it up some.

Proper dialogue punctuation is critical

When you write dialogue, you don't have to follow grammar rules because you're writing what your characters say, and people don't always use proper grammar when they speak. But you do have to follow a few dialogue punctuation rules.

Writing and punctuating dialogue is not easy, but doing a good job of this part of your writing is one of the most important parts of your writing.

Eight simple rules for punctuating dialogue

#1. Enclose dialogue in double quotation marks.

#2. Closing punctuation always goes to the left of the quotation marks. For example, the question mark or period always goes inside the closing quotation mark.

#3. When you change speakers, start a new paragraph.

#4. If your character is talking for more than one paragraph, you use opening quotes at the beginning of each paragraph but don't use closing quotes until after the end of the last paragraph.

#5. You won't need this rule much but use single quotes when the quoted material is within double quotes.

#6. If you're writing dialogue and the sentence continues after a tag, don't start the rest of the sentence with an upper-case letter.

#7. When you're formatting your manuscript, make sure you always use curly quotes and not straight quotes. Curly quotes will curve left or right, showing whether they're opening or closing quotation marks.

#8. Don't use a tag for every piece of dialogue. Dialogue tags are phrases and words such as *she said.* You want to use tags often enough so the reader always knows who's talking.

Miscellaneous tips for writing dialogue

- As a general rule, don't use long-winded dialogue. You can let your villain be a little long-winded at times, but give your readers the joy of seeing your hero shut him up sometimes with a short statement.

- Make your dialogue tight. After you write it, go back and delete as many words and sentences as possible.

- Introduce a few memorable lines—especially for your main character. One of the best ways to do this is to have them say something profound and unexpected.

- Don't use dialogue as an information dump by trying to tell your readers a lot of information all at once. People don't talk that way in real life—well, maybe a few people do, but they aren't your characters. Sprinkle in revealing comments to intrigue your readers and keep them turning the pages, but don't overload them with too much information all at once. Tell them more as the story moves along.

- You can use dialogue to reveal past events. For example,

as they were walking into the restaurant, Billy said, "Let's not mention anything about what happened Saturday night." This sets the stage for more information to be revealed about what happened Saturday night and will keep the readers turning pages.

- To improve your dialogue, get a friend to role-play with you. Each of you becomes a character. Read the dialogue you've written and see how it sounds. Where does it start to sound like it's not real? If someone overheard the two of you reading the dialogue, would they think you were having a conversation, or would they think you were reading a script?

The main takeaway from this chapter: A successful novel is impossible without believable and interesting dialogue. There are only a few rules for writing dialogue, but if you don't follow these rules, your readers will get distracted and confused. In most cases, dialogue is the heart of your story. Follow the instructions in this chapter, and you'll end up with some memorable, believable, and compelling dialogue you'll be proud of.

Chapter 14
Conflict and Climax

"Take chances. It may be bad, but it's the only way you can do anything really good."

~ William Faulkner

Conflict is the definition of a story. Without conflict, there is no story.

Your character has a goal, but he runs into some obstacles. That's conflict, and that's a story. Simply put:

Goal + obstacles = conflict

or

Desire + fear = conflict

In every conflict, there are stakes or things to lose. The higher the stakes, the greater the conflict.

The stakes may be as high as the character losing their life if they don't get out of the situation. Or the stakes may be failing a history exam if they go to the ball game instead of staying home and studying. The higher the stakes, the greater the conflict.

You want your character to experience many failures and setbacks. If they succeed all the time, your story won't be interesting. You need them to fail as much as (and maybe even more than) they succeed.

You've heard the old saying, "There's nothing to write home about." If that describes your story, you don't have a story—at least, you don't have a story anyone would want to read.

Whether you're writing a book about romance, crime, science fiction, a Western, or something else, your story will need to build to a climax where the main character finds himself in a more or less impossible situation.

A dude with a problem

Start your story by having a dude with a problem. Then, let your story build to a climax and then a resolution.

Your main character needs to have goals and experience conflicts, setbacks, and dilemmas. Decisions will need to be made, and there will probably be a disaster or two. Reactions to all these things will occur. How your main character deals with all of this is your story.

How are they ever going to get out of this? This is the point your story has been building up to. It's called the climax.

A story without conflict, problems, and then a great climax wouldn't be much of a story. The climax you write is the make-or-break moment in your story. If you have a ho-hum climax, you'll have a ho-hum story.

If you feel your story is falling flat and boring, it's most likely because of a lack of conflict. Readers love conflict.

Boring your readers is the cardinal sin of writers. You never want to bore your readers, no matter what. If a reader gets bored, they'll put your book down in a heartbeat.

You want to do the opposite. You want them to be so involved in your story that they forget to feed the cat.

Your story must have conflicts

We try to avoid conflicts in the real world, but we can't seem to get enough of them in the books we read.

Most people are happy to stay in their comfort zone and don't see the need to leave it until something smacks them upside the head. Something unexpected must come out of the blue and shock your hero into taking a risk and changing things in his world.

Your story will need both internal and external conflicts. There's a difference.

Internal and external conflicts

A simplified description of these two types of conflict is that external conflict is what happens, and internal conflict is why it matters.

External conflict is when something happens to the main character, such as his car won't start, a tornado is bearing down on him, or his cover has been blown when he's working undercover.

Internal conflict occurs when a person is facing a moral or spiritual dilemma or decision. For example, she is engaged, and the wedding date is two months away, but the love of her life, the guy she's had a crush on all through high school, has asked her to have dinner with him at a romanic restaurant.

Your main character (aka your hero) must have flaws if he's going to come across as real. Nobody is perfect. Even Superman had his weakness—kryptonite, which would deprive him of his powers.

Show—don't tell

What does this mean? It's an important point and something new writers screw up all the time. If you tell the readers the facts, they have nothing left to do to be involved in the story. You need to describe something happening and let the readers figure out the point you want to make.

Here are some examples:

- Instead of telling them that Bill was angry, say, "He picked up his phone and slammed the door as he bolted out of the room." Does this leave any doubt about whether Bill was angry or not?

- Don't say the kid was short. Say, "He had to stand on a stool to reach the refrigerator door handle."

- Don't say she was pretty. Say, "Every guy in the room stopped what they were doing and turned to look at her when she walked into a room with her long blonde hair swaying as she walked."

- Dialogue is another great way to show rather than tell the reader something. When you work information into the dialogue, the story can move along while you still get your point across.

- Let the reader deduce things rather than spoon-feeding them all the details.

- You want to give the reader an active role in experiencing your story. The best way to do this is to find ways to show them rather than telling them as much information as possible in your writing.

- Use an active voice rather than a passive voice in your writing. This one thing will make you sound like an experienced writer rather than a beginner.

- Don't over-explain things. Give your readers credit. They can figure the obvious things out for themselves.

- You can tell the reader something on rare occasions, but keep it brief and let the story move on.

You don't want to draw attention to your writing. Ideally, you want the reader to forget he's reading.

After all the conflict, there has to be a climax where everything looks hopeless, and then you reveal the unexpected resolution. You have to have all of this to have a good story.

The main takeaway from this chapter: Conflict is what your story is all about. Without conflict, there is no story. Readers love conflict. It keeps them involved in the story and turning the pages. Your readers have to care about your main character before they will care much about what happens to them, so make sure your readers have bonded with your main character before you start introducing conflict. And, of course, your story has to build to a climax and then end with a realistic but unexpected resolution.

Chapter 15
How to Write Endings

"If you want to be a writer, you must do two things above all others: read a lot and write a lot."

~ Stephen King

Are you wondering how to end your story? You want to write an unforgettable ending—but how do you pull that off in a powerful way?

All writers struggle with how to end their stories. Your ending should be memorable, profound, and definitely not predictable. If your readers don't remember the ending, they won't remember your book. You want to have an ending that will have them talking about your book and recommending it to their friends for weeks or months after they have read it.

You need a memorable ending

Write an ending that will leave a lasting impression on your readers. You don't want a predictable ending. If you've ever watched a Hallmark movie, you know they all end with the couple finally falling in love, their business is a success, and they live happily ever after.

It's okay to have a satisfying ending that your readers want, but you also need to throw a surprise in there. If you don't, your readers will forget your ending. They won't remember it, and they won't be telling their friends. You want readers to remember your book.

It's easy to kill off the bad guy or have the couple get married and end the book, but that's a cop-out. You can do better than that. Your readers probably saw that coming halfway through the book.

To have a good book, you will need to give your readers the ending they wanted and maybe saw coming but throw in a twist or surprise.

You have to wrap up all the loose ends unless you plan to write a sequel, and I recommend that you don't do that with your first book. If you leave anything that you brought up earlier unresolved, your readers will notice it. They won't like the book, and you will get bad reviews. It's that simple.

But even though you wrap up all loose ends, you want your readers to feel like your book is in the real world, and life goes on. There are still things the characters can do and want to do. Their lives don't end at the end of the book.

Here's how to pull off a powerful ending

You have to have a powerful climax and resolution to your novel. These are *not* the same thing.

The climax happens near the end of your book but not in the last chapter. The climax is the most intense time in your story. It's when the conflict comes to a head.

The resolution is when everything gets resolved. It happens in the last chapter. It's when everything settles down, and nothing is left up in the air.

This last chapter is the most important chapter in your book. It's the last impression your readers will have of your book. It will make or break your book.

Three ways to write great endings

1. **The explicit ending.** This is the easiest and most common way to end a book. In this type of ending, everything is wrapped up and clearly stated.

2. **The twist ending.** This makes a great and memorable ending if you can pull it off. Your readers will be saying, "I never saw that coming." You don't want this type of ending to come out of left field. Ideally, you would like for your readers to think, *I should have seen this coming, but I didn't.* In other words, it should be a logical and fitting ending to the story, but it was unexpected. A plot twist at the end of a horror story is common, but be careful if you have a plot twist at the end of a romance story.

3. **The tie-back ending.** This is an ending where everything is tied back to the beginning. This type of ending is popular for mysteries and thrillers. It makes everything that happened in the beginning make sense.

A few more comments about ending your story

Make sure everything is resolved—including the subplots. All of the subplots don't have to be resolved in the last chapter, but they do have to be resolved by the end of the book. Some things can be taken care of in earlier chapters.

Don't ever introduce a new character near the end of your story. For example, in a murder mystery, the killer can't be somebody you introduce near the end. It has to be somebody who has been around since the early part of the story. You would like for the reader to say, "I didn't see that coming."

Your resolution and ending need to be more than "They lived happily ever after," but don't drag it out over multiple chapters. The resolution/ending should be covered in one chapter, and it should be one of your shortest chapters. After everything is resolved, your story is over. Stop writing.

Your resolution should be clear and concise but don't make it too easy. You could end your story by killing off the bad guy or by saying it was all a dream, but that's too easy and not satisfying to the reader. Be more creative and come up with a better ending.

You've hooked the reader and pulled them into your story with the conflict. You have to make absolutely sure the ending fully resolves the conflict. Your readers are invested in your story and main character and are craving an ending.

How to tell if your book ending sucks

Ask yourself these four questions about the ending of your book. Unless you can answer "yes" to all of them, your ending sucks, and your readers will be disappointed and unhappy. Here are the questions:

#1. Do you have a satisfying resolution to the main conflict? You hooked the readers into reading your novel with an intriguing conflict. They've continued reading your book, and now you must deliver a satisfying resolution. It needs to be a clear ending that resolves the main conflict.

#2. Did you wrap up all of the loose ends? Even if you had a minor subplot way back in Chapter 3, you can't leave it hanging. You don't have to resolve all of the loose ends in the last chapter, but they must be resolved by the end of the book. When you find a subplot that has not been resolved, you may decide that it didn't add anything to your story and delete it instead of resolving it.

#3. Was your ending logical but unpredictable? You don't ever want an ending that the reader saw coming. The couple getting married, a child getting well from a dreaded illness, or the bad guy that nobody liked being found guilty of committing all the crimes are too predictable.

#4. Does your final paragraph leave your readers with the feeling you want them to have? When your readers finish your book, you want them to feel something. What do you want them to feel, and does your last paragraph give them that feeling?

How do your readers feel after finishing your book?

What do your readers feel after reading the final sentence of your book? Ask your beta readers how the ending made them *feel*. This is important. Listen carefully to the feedback you get from your beta readers when you ask them this question. Give considerable thought to your final sentence.

The beginning of your book is important to hook the reader and pull them into it. Most people don't remember how a book begins, but they sure remember how it ends. You want your book to have a memorable ending that will leave a lasting impression on your readers so they'll be telling their friends about your book.

Note: This chapter has mostly been about writing novel endings. The ending of a nonfiction book is important, too, but easier to write. It's simple to have a good ending for a nonfiction book. All you have to do is make sure to provide a clear solution to the problem your title and subtitle promised to solve. If the solution involves a series of steps, provide a summary. Don't leave the reader not knowing exactly what to do or with too many options.

The main takeaway from this chapter: The way you end your book is super important. I've read books I thought were pretty good until I got to the end, and then the author blew it. An ending that brings everything together and maybe has an unexpected twist will make the book memorable and one that readers will recommend to friends. When your ending does this, you've nailed it. The ending of your book is one of the main keys to its success.

Chapter 16
Rewriting, Editing, and Proofreading

"A writer is someone who has taught his mind to misbehave."

~ Oscar Wilde

You can never write a good book unless you let go of your inhibitions and let the words flow.

If you don't have a crappy first draft, it means you didn't let your words flow freely while you were writing. You were being too critical of your writing and trying to edit as you went along. The result will be a book that sounds stiff, artificial, and won't be enjoyable to read.

Turn your manuscript into a masterpiece

To do this, you'll need to rewrite sections of it several times and edit it extensively. Then, if you can afford one, you should turn it over to a professional proofreader.

I recommend Ken, who is known on Fiverr.com as mrproofreader. I have used his services for years. He is top-notch. You can find him on Fiverr.com at this link:

https://www.fiverr.com/mrproofreader

An editor would provide more help than a proofreader, but a good editor would cost you $2,000 to $3,000. A good proofreader is much less expensive. They charge about $250 to $350, depending on the length of your book.

I always use a proofreader, but I don't spend the money to hire an editor. I'm sure my books would be better if I also hired an editor, but I don't think my books would be sufficiently better to make the extra $2,000 to $3,000 investment worthwhile.

If you can't afford a professional proofreader, the next best option is to get a lot more beta readers. You don't pay beta readers.

Start by rewriting like mad

Writing your book is fun, but rewriting is hard work. After a day of rewriting, I sometimes feel like I've been run over by a dump truck. I'm mentally and physically drained. Rewriting will consist of deleting, rearranging, and rewording sections.

Everybody knows you can't proofread or edit your own work. At least, that's the conventional wisdom. But as I've said before, conventional wisdom is often wrong.

Start your rewriting process by letting your manuscript set for at least a week—two weeks would be even better. Start with the attitude that nothing is sacred. Cut sentences, paragraphs, and maybe even whole chapters. Cut out the fluff and rambling. This is called making your manuscript tight. If you have trouble getting a section to fit in, maybe it's because it doesn't belong there.

There's a phrase writers use called "Kill your darlings." It means sometimes you'll have sections you love and are proud of and feel like they're profound, but then when you look back and reread them, you realize they shouldn't be there. But they're so good you don't want to get rid of them. Delete the sections anyway. In other words, "Kill your darlings."

Your manuscript won't be perfect when you finish editing it. Heck, it wouldn't be perfect if you had hired a professional proofreader and editor. I'm calling it a manuscript because I don't consider it a book until after publication.

Make good use of beta readers

The more people you can get to be what is called a beta reader to read your manuscript and give you their feedback, the better. No one person, not even the professionals, will catch all the mistakes in your manuscript.

You don't want friends who will stroke your ego and tell you how great your book is—your mother will do that. You want people who will read your manuscript carefully and be ruthless and supercritical.

You will need at least three or four beta readers—a dozen would be even better. Remember that some people who promise to read your manuscript will never get around to it.

They probably had good intentions, but life gets in the way, and sometimes, things come up in their lives that are more important to them than reading your manuscript.

How about your English teacher or some other teachers? Could you get them to read your manuscript? By all means, ask. If you know any authors, ask them to read your manuscript. Ask a lot of people.

Don't feel obligated to make all the changes your beta readers recommend. Some of the recommended changes are to fix errors, but some of them will be recommendations on how they think you can say something better. Consider all the suggestions, but it's your book. You want it to be your voice.

How to edit your own writing

Here's how you can go against conventional wisdom and edit your own book. Do this before you give your manuscript to your proofreader or beta readers. You don't want them to know how bad your first draft was.

Editing can be frustrating and emotionally draining, but if you remove the emotions, it becomes a series of logical steps.

You'll find errors after the book is published

This is not as big of a deal as it used to be. You can log on to Amazon, and with a few keystrokes and at zero cost, you can make changes to your book's eBook and print versions. Then, when someone orders either version of your book the next day, they'll receive the corrected copy.

Amazon does what's called "print-on-demand," and they don't print a book until someone orders it, but they still usually ship it the same day.

Here's my secret technique for finding errors in my manuscript

The technique is simple—**have your computer read your manuscript aloud to you.** I call this technique a secret because almost nobody uses it, but it works wonders.

It works so well because your mind knows what the words are trying to say, and your subconscious mind will insert missing words or change words, and your brain will hear what your manuscript was trying to say.

Have MS Word, LibreOffice, or another computer program use a text-to-voice feature to read your manuscript to you as you follow along, looking at the printed text. I've never failed to find errors when I do this. It's important that you follow along, looking at the text as you hear the words read aloud to you.

If you don't already have a text-to-voice program on your computer, you can search Google for free programs. You'll find plenty of them.

When should you stop editing?

Your book will never be perfect, but you can't keep tweaking it forever. If you're fixing mistakes, that's fine, but sometimes, you'll find yourself making changes because you think it sounds better. You may be doing more harm than good. The more changes you make, the less the book will sound like you.

I read a book not long ago that was published by a major publishing company. The book said Death Valley was in Nevada. The last time I was there, it was in California. Almost all books have errors in them.

When you edit your manuscript, look for factual errors. Proofreaders and beta readers are not skilled at finding factual mistakes, and they're usually not even looking for them. They're also probably not experts on the topic of your book, so don't expect them to find all of the factual errors in your book. That's your job.

At some point, you will have to decide that your manuscript is "good enough" to publish.

If you don't feel like your book is ready to publish yet

If you want your book to be closer to perfect before you spend a lot of money hiring an editor, consider investing $3.99 to get the eBook version of a book I recently wrote called ***Book Editing Guide: How to Edit Your First Book.*** Here's a link to it on Amazon.

https://www.amazon.com/dp/194702020X

But if you follow what I've said in this chapter and use your beta readers effectively, you can get by without this book.

The main takeaway from this chapter: Don't stop with an okay editing job. Transform your messy first draft into a polished book that you'll be proud to put your name on. The techniques described in this chapter will make that happen. The most important key to rewriting, editing, and proofreading your manuscript is getting as many beta readers as possible to read it and give you their feedback. Beta readers are necessary even if you have used a professional proofreader.

Chapter 17

How to Write a Nonfiction Book

"Nonfiction is never going to die."

~ Tom Wolfe

A nonfiction book (or a "how-to" book as it's sometimes called) is totally different from a novel.

So far, I've mainly discussed writing fiction (with a few comments about writing nonfiction thrown in). This chapter is devoted entirely to showing you how to write nonfiction.

One thing that makes writing a nonfiction book easier than writing fiction is that you don't have to always keep the whole story in your head. In a nonfiction book, each chapter more or less stands alone.

Even though a nonfiction book is easier to write, many authors say writing a novel is more fun. When writing a novel, you can use your imagination and take your book in any direction you find interesting.

The purpose of a novel is to entertain the readers, while the goal of a nonfiction book is to solve a problem for the readers. They are two different animals.

You may think you don't have enough knowledge or experience about any topic or problem to write a nonfiction book describing a solution that will solve the readers' problem, but look at it this way.

Your own knowledge or research?

All nonfiction books are a combination of the writer's knowledge, experience, and research. It may be 90% knowledge and experience and 10% research or vice versa. In the end, the reader doesn't care where the information came from as long as it has the solution to their problem.

For example, I didn't do much research when I wrote books about living the RVing lifestyle or being a digital nomad. Instead, I based the books mostly on my experience.

However, when I wrote the two books *Book Marketing Magic* and *Book Editing Guide*, a ton of research was required. I knew a lot about these topics, but I wanted the books to include everything that was known in the industry about the topics. I read almost every book on Amazon and watched every YouTube video discussing these subjects.

If you want to write a nonfiction book, pick a topic you're interested in and one you will enjoy doing research into. Add what you learn from your research to what you already know, and you will have the information to write a great book. It doesn't matter that 90% of the information in your book came from research. After all, by the time you finish doing your research and writing your book, you will be an expert on the topic.

A nonfiction book is easier to write and market than a novel

The best part about a nonfiction book compared to a novel is that it's so much easier to market a nonfiction book. It's also easier to write, but maybe not as enjoyable.

When people have a problem, they often search Amazon using keyword phrases describing their problem or the solution. They don't use this technique when they're looking for a novel to read. They may search for a category or their favorite author but not for keyword phrases.

To sell your nonfiction book, you must have a title and subtitle that boldly promises that your book has the solution to the readers' problem. You must also ensure your title and subtitle include the keyword phrases the readers will search for. Amazon gives you seven keyword slots to add even more keywords and phrases.

One important point. Your nonfiction book absolutely has to deliver on the strong, bold promise you made in your title and subtitle.

I wrote two books about how to write a nonfiction book, and I can't begin to cover all the details in this one chapter that were included in those two books, but I want to give you the important points.

If you want to know more about this topic, check out my book *How to Start Writing Your Book Today: A Step-By-Step Guide to Nonfiction.* The eBook is only $3.99, and it's available from Amazon at this link:

https://www.amazon.com/dp/1947020218

Steps to writing a nonfiction book

Writing a nonfiction book is different from writing a novel. Here are the steps you need to follow to write your nonfiction book:

First, you need to select a topic. It needs to be one you're interested in, but it also needs to be one several other people are interested in so you can sell a lot of books. The way you find out how interested other people are in your topic is to see how many times a month people search Amazon for the keyword phrases describing the problem your book promises to solve.

Knowing which keywords and phrases get a lot of searches each month on Amazon (without much competition) is the most valuable information you can have to help you write, publish, and sell a nonfiction book.

Let me give you an example. The keyword phrase *guide book* gets 6,199 searches a month. My grammar program says it should be one word, but the single-word *guidebook* gets only 634 monthly searches.

How do I know this? It's simple. I use a program called Publisher Rocket that tells me how many searches any word or phrase gets each month on Amazon, how competitive it is, the other books ranking for the phrase, how much money each of those books is making a month, and a ton of other information.

It's also useful for writing novels, but it's a must-have tool if you want to write a nonfiction book that will sell well and make money. It's not a free program, but for a one-time investment of $97, you get lifetime access to it, including all the updates. Go to their website and see what this program can do for you and how much easier it is to write your nonfiction book when you're using this tool.

Here is my affiliate link to the Publisher Rocket program:

https://www.aLaptopLife.com/rocket

Before you start writing your nonfiction book, you need to come up with a title and subtitle. To see if other people are interested in your topic, come up with a dozen or more keyword phrases you think people would be searching for if they were interested in the solution you will be providing. Be sure to use your most-searched-for keyword phrases in your title and subtitle. Your title and subtitle will promise a solution to the readers' problem. You need to know what you promised before you can start writing your book and delivering that solution. Keywords and titles are not as important for a novel as they are for a nonfiction book.

You need to select profitable keywords and phrases for your title and subtitle.

Create a table of contents that shows the title of each chapter. Think of this as your outline. It shows the topics you'll cover in your book. I read over my table of contents almost every time I sit down to write. I add, delete, and rearrange the chapters often.

Most of the time, the chapters in novels don't have a title other than the chapter number, but sometimes they do have a title. Either way is acceptable.

Now you're ready to start writing your book

You don't have to start by trying to write the first line of your first chapter. If you try to do that, you may get hung up and stare at a blank page for hours.

Pick out the chapter you're most passionate about. Even then, you don't necessarily need to start writing the beginning of the chapter. Start writing the part you're the most enthusiastic about, and let the words flow.

Now you're writing. When you're staring at a blank page trying to come up with a powerful opening line, you're not writing—you're thinking about writing.

The easy way to write your nonfiction book is to pretend you're sitting across the kitchen table talking to a friend who has asked you how to do whatever your book is about.

It's okay to ramble, discuss things out of order, and leave out some points. You can return and add these later. Imagine that you are talking to your friends and telling them things as the points come to mind. When you go back, fill in the blanks about the information you left out. When you're editing, you can put your points in order.

When talking to a friend, you won't worry if you didn't describe the steps in order or rambled too much. You would just talk. That's the way you should write your first draft.

If you're having trouble writing your thoughts down, maybe you could try talking to a friend and recording the conversation. Then, later, transcribe what you said, and you will be well on your way to having a first draft of that chapter. Repeat this for the next chapter if the technique works for you. I prefer to type as I think but do whatever works for you.

How to write without feeling any stress

Don't get bent out of shape and frustrated trying to write your first draft. Remember the words of the famous English author Terry Pratchett. He said, *"The first draft is just you telling yourself the story."*

Keeping this thought in mind will relieve pressure and make it easier to write the first draft of your story—whether you're writing a novel or a nonfiction book.

The main takeaway from this chapter: Some of the steps and techniques involved in writing a nonfiction book are the same or similar to those involved in writing a novel, but not all of them. In this chapter, I've tried to point out what you will be doing differently when writing a nonfiction book.

The techniques and writing process for writing a good nonfiction book are different. Many famous authors change hats and write both fiction and nonfiction books. You can, too. Maybe you should write one of each and see which one you enjoy the most. If you decide to do that, you'll have the problem of deciding which one you want to write first.

Chapter 18

Formatting and Publishing Your Book

"I had 122 rejection slips before I sold a story."

~ F. Scott Fitzgerald

Now that you've written your book, you're ready for the fun part—publishing it.

But first, you have to format it. You have to submit a PDF version to Amazon for the printed book and an ePub version for the eBook. Amazon no longer accepts a mobi-formatted version.

Three ways to format your manuscript for Amazon

#1. I use the Atticus.io writing program, and I can download the manuscript in PDF, ePub, or docx format with the click of a button. This program will cost you $145, but you can use it to write your book and then reformat it as many times as you want. This is a good option if you plan to write more than one book. I like that the program is easy to use and gives you several templates, so you have a lot of ways to format your book.

#2. If you wrote your book using MS Word or LibreOffice (a free program similar to Word), several videos on YouTube will show you how to convert a docx file to a PDF and an ePub file.

#3. As a last resort, several people on Fiverr.com will format your manuscript and send you versions that are ready to submit to Amazon for about $50. I used to do this all the time until I bought the Atticus.io program.

After your book is formatted, you're ready to submit it to Amazon

You can publish your book today using Amazon. It's fast, easy, and free. Your book will be in your hands in a matter of days, and you no longer have to worry about finding an agent or getting a publisher to publish it.

In this chapter, I will show you step-by-step how to publish your eBook and printed book on Amazon.

When you first consider all the steps necessary to publish your book on Amazon, it might seem like a complicated process, but it's not. It's just a lot of simple steps. In this chapter, I'll go over them one by one.

Publish your eBook first

Go to kdp.amazon.com, the Kindle Direct Publishing website. If you already have an account, click the "**Sign-in**" button. If not, click the "**Sign-up**" button to set one up.

You'll need to provide Amazon with your banking and tax information. If you're setting up a personal account, they'll need your Social Security number, and if you're setting up a business account, your business tax ID number.

After your account is set up, log in and start submitting information about your book to Amazon.

Start by clicking on the "**Bookshelf**" button and then the yellow "**Create**" button. Next, click on the "**Kindle eBook**" box below the words "**Create a New Title.**"

Be sure you're happy with your title because after your book is published, you can change everything else about your book except the title, subtitle, and author's name.

Keep filling in the boxes

After you've entered the title, keep going. Everything else in the process is pretty simple. You just keep filling in the boxes.

Here are a few comments about some of the boxes that might be a little confusing.

The first box asks you to provide a description of your book. If you've already written it, copy and paste it into the box provided by Amazon. If you haven't formatted it, you can use the tools at the top of the box to make some of the text larger and some bold, add bullets, etc. You can type it directly in the description box if you haven't written your description.

It's important to note that your book description should *not* be a description of your book but rather a write-up to convince the reader to buy it.

You don't want your description to be one long paragraph. No one will read it. You need to make the first line bold and larger type, have some bullets, and include several short paragraphs. End your description with a call to action.

The next step is to fill in the seven keyword slots. Enter keyword phrases rather than a single keyword in these boxes. No one searches Amazon for a single word.

Keyword phrases are especially important for nonfiction books because most readers will find books by searching for keywords that describe their problems.

Amazon allows you to have 50 characters (and that includes spaces) in each of the seven keyword boxes. Put your most important keyword phrases in the first slots and put only one keyword phrase in each slot for your most important keyword phrases. You can include multiple keyword phrases (up to the 50-character limit) for your last two or three boxes. Don't put a comma between the phrases. When you include more than one keyword phrase in a slot, Amazon doesn't value it as highly as when there's only one phrase, but inserting multiple keyword phrases will get your book indexed for more phrases.

Don't use any keyword phrases you used in your title or subtitle in your keyword boxes. It won't hurt anything, but it's a waste since Amazon will already index the words in the title and subtitle.

If you need help finding the best keywords for your book, check out the Publisher Rocket tool. My affiliate link is shown below.

https://www.aLaptopLife.com/rocket

Check it out and see how you can increase your book sales. It will help you select keywords and the best categories for your book.

Selecting categories

Next is the category section. Selecting the right categories is important if you've written a novel because many times, people search for fiction books by categories.

Categories are less important for a nonfiction book because readers search Amazon for keywords rather than categories when looking for a book to buy to solve their problem, but they are important for a novel.

Selecting the three categories involves a few steps, but they are straightforward. Keep jumping through hoops, and you'll get there.

The instructions in the box make it easy to go through the steps and find the categories where your book would best fit. Be sure to drill down and find the subcategories for your book. Don't list it in a broad category, such as history or boats. You can use the Publisher Rocket program to find the categories that don't have many competitors.

If your book is not a children's book, leave the next section about the age range blank. It doesn't apply to your book.

After you have completed everything on the first page, click the yellow "**Save and Continue**" box at the bottom. This will take you to the next page, which will start by discussing **Digital Rights Management (DRM).**

I always click on "**No**" for DRM. If you want to learn more details about this, click on "**How is my Kindle eBook affected by DRM?**" Then you can see a detailed explanation. Note that you can't change this after you publish your book. You're making progress. Keep going.

Next, upload your manuscript

For your eBook, you will need to upload your manuscript in ePub format.

If you have included any photos in your manuscript, make sure you compress them in your eBook. Amazon charges you a delivery fee for every eBook you sell based on the file size, and if you have a lot of uncompressed photos, this could add up. When someone is reading an eBook, a compressed and an uncompressed photo looks the same.

Note that later, when you upload the print version of your book, you'll upload it in a PDF format. I'll cover the details of this later in the chapter. For now, there are a few more things you need to do to finish publishing your eBook.

Your eye-catching cover

The next thing you will do is upload your eBook cover. Upload the cover you have already had someone design for you. Don't click on the yellow "**Launch Cover Creator**" button. If you go that route, you could end up with a lousy cover.

You can change the cover after your book is printed, but take the time to make sure you have an attention-grabbing cover now.

Click on the circle and select "**Upload a cover you already have.**" Your eBook cover must be in PDF or TIFF format, not JPEG.

You're making progress

We're getting closer. There are a lot of steps, but they're all easy. So, let's keep going.

Next, click "**Launch Previewer.**" Amazon converts the files at its own slow pace. This usually takes several minutes, so be patient.

After Amazon has converted the files, take your time and use the previewer to scroll through your book. Be sure every page is exactly as you want it to be, and make sure all the links—if you have included any—are clickable. Don't rush the process of thoroughly checking your book. You want it to be right. You can correct any part later, but try your best to get it right the first time.

After checking everything, the next box is where you can enter an ISBN, but since an eBook doesn't require one, leave this box blank.

You're almost finished

Now click the yellow "**Save and Continue**" button to proceed to the last page of the eBook submission process.

Check the box "**Enroll my book in KDP Select**." You can read about it on Amazon and change your selection later, but for now, take my word for it, check this box, and move on.

For territories, select "**All territories**," and for your "Primary Marketplace," select "**Amazon.com**" if you are in the United States.

Now, it's time to set your price. Click on the **70%** circle. To qualify for the 70% commission, you must set your price between $2.99 and $9.99. You might want to set your price at $0.99 or even $0.00 for the first few days as part of your marketing strategy. If you do this, you must click on the 30% circle. (Note: It takes a whole book to discuss book marketing strategies. That's what I cover in my recent book, *Book Marketing Magic*.)

For the final price of your eBook (after the promotion period), I've found the sweet spot to be $2.99 for novels and $3.99

for nonfiction books, but you can experiment and change your price from time to time to find your most profitable price.

The book lending option is selected automatically when you select the 70% commission option.

At the bottom of the page, click on the circle that says, "**I am ready to publish my book now**."

Finally, you can click the yellow "**Publish Your Kindle eBook**" button.

Congratulations, you've published your eBook

You will see a note at the bottom of the page that says it could take up to 72 hours for your title to be available for purchase on Amazon. My experience is that the eBook will usually be available in less than 24 hours.

I buy a copy as soon as my eBook is available for purchase. I always read it cover to cover and click on all the links as a final check to ensure everything is correct. (I sometimes find formatting and other errors.)

Another reason to buy a copy of your book is that Amazon doesn't start ranking a book until there has been at least one sale.

Now publish the print version

Before you submit your print book to Amazon, it must be formatted and saved as a PDF file.

You'll have to select the size of your book and set the margins. The inside and outside margins are usually set differently. Here are the numbers I use when I'm formatting my print books.

All my books are 6" by 9", and I set the inside margins at 0.825 and the outside margins at 0.625. The inside margin needs to be a little wider to accommodate the binding. Play with the margins to see what you like. I set the font size at 12 points.

You can start the submission process after your manuscript is formatted and saved as a PDF file.

It's similar to submitting your eBook. You have to check a lot of boxes and jump through several hoops. Many steps are the same, but a few things will be different from your eBook submission process.

Publishing a printed book is different

The cover you submit will be different. It will need a front cover, back cover, and spine all in one file. If you have hired an experienced book cover designer to design your cover, they will send you the file ready for you to submit to Amazon.

You must select whether you want your cover to be matt or glossy. I always choose glossy covers because they look more professional, and some authors tell me they choose matt for the same reason.

You have to select white paper or cream paper. I always go with the white paper. I like it better. When you're having your cover designed, you'll have to tell your designer whether you will be using white paper or cream paper. There is a slight difference in the thickness of the paper, which will affect the thickness of the spine. Cream might also clash with or complement the colors on your cover.

You have to have an ISBN to sell your book on Amazon. When you get to where Amazon asks you to enter your ISBN, click the box that says, "**Assign me a free KDP ISBN**." Amazon will give you an ISBN at no charge. That's what I suggest you do. The disadvantage of letting Amazon supply your ISBN instead of buying your own is that when Amazon furnishes your ISBN, you can only sell your book on Amazon. I don't sell my books through any other outlet anyway.

To summarize, I always select no-bleed and white paper for the pages instead of cream and glossy paper instead of matt for the cover.

I usually price my print books at $13.95 or $14.95. I've experimented with different prices, but that seems to be the sweet spot. I like to price my print books to earn about $5.00 for each book.

As soon as the book is available for sale, I purchase it at retail price and check it thoroughly. Don't be surprised if you find an error or two—I almost always do. Changing the manuscript and resubmitting the corrected book to Amazon in minutes is easy. Pay special attention to the formatting. Make sure your book looks the way you want it to look.

The main takeaway from this chapter: There are a lot of steps involved in publishing a book on Amazon, but none of them are complicated. Keep jumping through the hoops, and you'll get it done. Don't worry about making a mistake. Amazon checks your work and will tell you if you need to change something. You can change almost anything, even after your book is printed.

Chapter 19

Lost, Confused, or Overwhelmed? Start Here

"You know what I did after I wrote my first novel? I shut up and wrote twenty-three more."

~ Michael Connelly

I have provided extensive information about how to write your book. Maybe I've given you too much to comprehend all at one time.

A writer friend of mine once told me he sometimes thinks he should put his quill back in the goose where it would be more useful. It's normal to feel lost, confused, or overwhelmed at times.

These feelings are common whether you're writing a novel or a nonfiction book, but they will be different depending on the type of book you're writing.

Maybe I should have a chapter for each type of book, but I'm going to lump everything together in this one chapter because they are the same feelings—but the causes and cures are a little different. I'll point out the differences as I go along in the chapter. Let's get started.

What should you do first?

There are so many ways to start writing your book that it's easy to get completely overwhelmed. Maybe you feel like you're experiencing information overload.

You don't want to start writing a book unless you're sure you'll finish it and that it will be a book you'll be proud to put your name on.

Almost all writers feel a little lost when they're getting ready to start writing a book.

Since you've read this far in the book, I know you're dead serious about writing your book. The good news is that now you know more about how to write and publish a book than most people who have written one. You probably don't have the confidence yet, but you definitely have the knowledge.

An overview of how to start writing your book

1. **If you're going to write a nonfiction book, first decide on a topic.** You may already have a topic you want to write about for your first book, but before you put a lot of time and effort into writing your book, take the time to make sure the topic is not too broad. If you're thinking about writing about traveling, dieting, or building a boat, those topics are too broad. Consider writing about a narrow niche of one of those topics. For example: What kind of boat are you describing how to build? Where or how will you be traveling? What kind of diet? And think about what new information your book will include that the other books haven't already covered.

2. **If you're going to write a novel, consider starting without**

an outline. Start by thinking about the general idea of your plot, where the story is going to take place and give some thought to your characters—particularly your main character. Let the story start coming together and developing in your head. Don't expect to come up with all the answers in one sitting. Your story's path and ending may differ greatly from what you thought when you started writing it. After all, the main character is telling the story. You're just writing down what he says and does. You're telling his story.

3. **Select your writing software tool.** Any job is easier when you have the right tools. You'll need a software writing tool. You may already have MS Word (or a similar free program, LibreOffice) on your computer. The three other popular book-writing programs (listed in the order of popularity) are Vellum, Atticus.io, and Scrivener. I like (and use) Atticus.io because it's the easiest to learn and use and has several features that make writing easier. It also allows me to quickly format my book and export versions formatted as eBooks (ePub) and printed books (PDF) ready to submit to Amazon. I always find errors and things I want to change after I publish my books. With Atticus.io, I can make the changes (reformat the book) and resubmit it to Amazon in a few minutes.

4. **Decide on keyword phrases:** If you're writing a nonfiction book, you'll need these for your title, subtitle, and seven keyword slots. Amazon will make these seven keyword slots available to you in publication. Before you start writing, you need to know what your keyword phrases are so you can be sure to work them into your manuscript. You don't want to waste time trying to get ranked for a keyword phrase that's not discussed or even

mentioned in your book.

5. **Create a title (and if you're writing a nonfiction book, a subtitle).** This is the next step after you've come up with your keyword phrases. Don't skip this step. Your title and subtitle are important to the success of your nonfiction book. Readers search for nonfiction books using keyword phrases, so it's important to have the keywords and keyword phrases they will be searching for in the title and subtitle of your nonfiction book.

6. **Hire someone to design the eBook cover for your book.** You can't have the cover for the print version designed yet because you don't know how many pages your book will have, so you don't know how thick to make the spine. Having a working version of your front cover designed before you start doing much writing is important. Post your book cover at the top of your manuscript so you'll see it every time you sit down to write. It will keep you motivated. Don't be afraid to make changes to your cover as you write your book.

7. **Create your table of contents if you're writing a nonfiction book:** This is where you get creative and where your book will take on its own life and show how it's different from other books on the same subject. Readers can (and many will) read your table of contents before deciding to buy your book. They can see it when they click on the "**Read Sample**" button below the book on Amazon's detail page. You need to look at the table of contents of the books you'll be competing with, not to copy what they've done but to see what topics they're covering and help you decide how your book is going to be different. What new information or techniques will be in your book?

Novels don't usually have chapter titles, but if you're writing a nonfiction book, make your chapter titles intriguing and enticing so readers will want to read each chapter. This will help you sell your book and encourage people to keep reading after buying it. If they finish reading your book, they're more likely to leave you a review. Also, if they don't finish reading your nonfiction book, they won't benefit from your profound solution to their problem. After all, most people buy a nonfiction book to solve a problem.

And if they don't finish reading your novel, they won't see your fantastic ending, so they're not likely to recommend your book to their friends.

When I write a nonfiction book, I add and delete chapters, change chapter titles, and rearrange the chapters throughout the writing process. In a way, your table of contents is an outline.

If you're writing a novel, consider not using an outline and letting the main character take over the story. Some writers use an outline when writing a novel. Even if you're not using an outline, you may find having one for one or two difficult chapters helpful. Go with whatever works for you.

Now you're ready to start writing—here's how you do it

Writing your manuscript will be much easier after you've completed the tasks I've described in this chapter. With these completed, you've already done a lot of writing and accomplished some of the hardest parts of the book-writing process. From this point on, when you sit down to write, you won't have to worry about where to start or what to write next.

To get started, select the chapter you're most passionate about (for a nonfiction book) and start there. If you're writing a novel, start with the scene that intrigues you the most.

Put a lot of effort into your first chapter

Go back and read and tweak this chapter often while you're writing your book.

This is the most important chapter in your book, but it doesn't necessarily need to be the first chapter you start writing.

If it's a nonfiction book, in the first chapter, you need to convince the reader that you understand their problem and have the knowledge and experience to solve it uniquely.

If your book is a novel, you need to hook the reader and pull them into the story in the first chapter.

As you continue writing your book, review the first chapter, edit it, and rewrite sections occasionally.

When you start writing, don't worry about whether you're doing a good job or not. Let your mind go, and just write. After all, you may end up deleting what you wrote in the beginning anyway.

After you write one chapter, pick out the next chapter or scene you're passionate about and work on that one. Continue this process. You don't even have to finish a chapter or scene before you start writing the next one. Your goal now is to put words on the page (or computer screen). You can edit, rewrite, delete, and rearrange sections later.

Write as if you were sitting and talking to one person. Never write like you're speaking to a group.

Follow the steps outlined in this chapter, and you'll never feel confused or overwhelmed when you're writing your book.

Even if you have only an hour a day to write, if you follow the steps described in this book, you'll be able to write, rewrite, edit, proofread, and publish your book and have a copy in your hand in a few months. Keep that thought in your mind as you work on writing your profound book.

One final point: If you think you can't write a book, stop and ask yourself which of the things I've listed in this chapter it is that you think you can't do. I'm sure the magnitude of the whole project is what has you overwhelmed, not any one thing. When you break it into small parts, it's doable.

The main takeaway from this chapter: Almost everything I've told you in this chapter goes against conventional wisdom, but if you do what I've described, you will end up writing and publishing a book that you'll be proud of, and it won't take you long to make it happen.

Chapter 20
Closing Comments

"Our life is frittered away by detail. Simplify, simplify."

~ Henry David Thoreau

I know you're serious about writing and publishing a book. If you weren't, you would have stopped reading this book way before you got this far. You now have the knowledge you need to write and publish your book. All you have to do is make it happen.

You can start today and have your book written, edited, proofread, and published, and hold a copy in your hands in less than 90 days. Think about the feelings you'll experience when you have that book in your hands.

I've covered a lot of material in this book. You can't expect to remember everything. When you're working on each part of your book, go back and reread the chapter in this book that discusses that topic.

Whether you're describing your characters or writing dialogue, take the time to read the chapter again about how to do that. No one is going to know how many times you reread each chapter, but they will know what a great job you did writing your book.

As Ernest Hemingway said, "It's none of their business that you had to learn to write. Let them think you were born that way."

When you write and publish your first book, you will have accomplished what a New York Times article said 81% of the people in the US say they want to do. They say they want to write a book, but less than 1% of them will ever do it. And not many of the people who write a book will ever take the next step and publish it.

Your goal is to write and publish a book

Your goal shouldn't be to publish a perfect book. Give it your best effort. Publish a book you'll be proud of, but get it done.

The world is full of people who are working on a book. Most of them will never finish their book. Don't let that be you.

The good news is that revising and republishing a book is now so easy. I can make changes to my manuscript, log in to Amazon, and republish the book within 10 minutes. After I make the changes, the next person who orders the eBook or the printed book will receive the revised version. And there's no cost for me to do this.

Make your book a reality

The way to make your book a reality is to start writing it before you're ready.

Start writing your book today. You're more motivated now than you'll ever be. If you don't take the first steps and start writing your book today, face the fact that you'll probably never write your book.

You can start writing your book right now. I know you're probably thinking you're not ready, but you have to get started before you're ready. Give up trying to find the perfect time to write your book. You will never even find a good time to write, and, for sure, you'll never find the perfect time.

The world is waiting for your book

Amazon publishes over two million new books every year. But none of the authors have your unique knowledge, writing style, or flair. They can't even come close to writing the book you could write.

You're more prepared and motivated now than you'll ever be. If you don't start writing your book today, you will likely never write it. Let that sink in.

Imagine what your friends, family, and teachers will think about you when you've written and published a book. Almost everyone would like to be an author and have a published book with their name on it, but you will have done it.

Write one sentence today

Write one sentence today, and you'll be on your way to finishing your book. Don't try to write a killer first sentence—do that later. Today, all you want to do is write one sentence.

After you do that, why not write a few more sentences? Don't worry if you think what you're writing is not any good. It's probably not, and you'll likely delete it later, but your goal for today is not to write something good. Your goal is to start writing.

You read this book to learn how to write and publish a book. Maybe you didn't buy this book. Maybe somebody gave it to you because they believed in you and knew you could write a book if you knew how to do it. Now you do.

The main takeaway from this chapter: Now that you know how to write a book and how easy it will be, don't keep the world waiting for your earth-shattering, entertaining, and fantastic book. Start writing your book today, and you can hold it in your hands in a few weeks.

Remember, spending $10 and getting your eBook cover designed will almost guarantee that your book will be written and published. I've never seen a book not get written and published when the author had a book cover designed before they did much writing.

Chapter 21
Did You Like This Book?

If you liked this book, I would appreciate it if you would take a minute and post a short review on Amazon.

Everyone is super busy these days, and fewer than one person out of a hundred will take the time to post a review. Maybe that's why Amazon values reviews so highly and ranks books high if they have a lot of reviews.

I read and appreciate every review.

Here's the easy way to post a review:

Search Amazon for the title of this book. Here it is:

Book Writing Guide for Teens

This will take you to the book's detail page on Amazon. Scroll about halfway down the page until you see the yellow bar graph on the left side. Then click on the box below the graph that says, "Write a customer review." (It's the box the arrow is pointing to in the following screenshot.)

Next, click on the number of stars, and then go to the box that says, **"Add a written review,"** and type one or two sentences. Then go up to where it says, **"Add a headline,"** add a headline, click on **"Submit,"** and you're all finished. It's that simple.

Posting your review will take less than a minute and mean the world to me.

Writing an Amazon review is not like writing a high school book report. It's not a review of the whole book. It's a comment on one thing you liked about the book, found interesting, or learned from the book. That's all you have to say.

It's not so important what the review says—not many people read the reviews anyway—but they do look at the total number of reviews. So, the important thing is to post a review.

The main takeaway from this chapter: If you post a review, I'll be eternally grateful—or at least I'll be grateful for a long, long time.

Chapter 22
About the Author

Jerry Minchey is the author of 30 books. He has a bachelor's degree in electrical engineering, an MBA from USC, an OPM degree from Harvard Business School, and he holds five patents.

In his early career, he worked for NASA and later for many years as a computer design engineer before starting his own engineering and marketing company, which he ran for 20+ years.

He has a private pilot license with an instrument rating.

He lives six months out of the year in his motorhome, mainly in the North Carolina Mountains and Florida, and six months in Costa Rica.

His main hobbies are hiking to waterfalls, traveling, and writing. He used to be active in ham radio—KB4LL—but that's not easy to do while living and traveling in a motorhome. He likes to play bluegrass banjo and old-time fiddle, but playing those hasn't gotten much attention lately. He's also trying to get better with his Spanish so he can enjoy more conversations with the locals when he's in Costa Rica.

He is the owner and editor of two websites:

LifeRV.com

aLaptopLife.com.

Made in United States
Orlando, FL
25 April 2024

46179357R00075